ℓc

Kings and Priests

"Kings and Priests"

The "Universal Priesthood of Believers," Presented on the Basis of Holy Writ

By
R. C. H. Lenski

1927
THE LUTHERAN LITERARY BOARD
BURLINGTON, IOWA

THIS LITTLE VOLUME
IS FOR ALL THOSE WHOM
OUR LORD AND SAVIOR JESUS CHRIST
HAS MADE

KINGS AND PRIESTS

UNTO HIMSELF
BY HIS WORD AND GRACE

May It Help Them to Believe, Confess, Labor and Die
as befits men with royal and priestly hearts
to the glory of their

ETERNAL KING AND HIGH PRIEST

AMEN

TABLE OF CONTENTS

A Glance at the Titles

A good many Christian believers may be surprised when first they find themselves graced with the lofty titles

KINGS AND PRIESTS

on the sacred pages of the Bible. It may seem to them that such titles can only be figures of speech, like roses placed in our hands, or wreaths upon our heads, neither of which are part of our being, both of which soon wither and must be thrown away. Yet a little investigation shows that this view is wrong — these titles are meant literally.

In fact, when a comparison is made with the kings and priests ordinarily known among men we soon see that our Christian kingship and priesthood as believers in Christ Jesus is a far higher, truer, and more genuine thing than any royal or sacerdotal office otherwise known among men. It is a great and glorious biblical fact — we are indeed "kings and priests unto God and his (Christ's) Father"!

It is the same with all the other titles given to us as believers in the Bible. They are all real, never mere figures of speech. For instance, we are called "sons of God," "the children of God," members of the household of God, if sons then heirs. These designations express realities. For we are indeed born anew of incorruptible seed. God is actually our Father. Christ calls us his brethren. and we are that and nothing less. Our wonderful rights as children as well as our "inheritance incorruptible and undefiled and that fadeth not away" are described at length. The same thing is true of the other titles in the Bible: we are "friends" of Jesus, his "disciples," his "servants," "laborers," "stewards," etc. Every term expresses a reality, and is thus genuine and true in the highest degree. Some of these titles, like "disciples" and "servants," have come into constant use among Christians, and therefore seem more familiar than the two placed at the head of this little volume. But this does not make the latter any less genuine and true.

It belongs to the credit of Luther and the work of the Reformation that the great spiritual realities of the royal priesthood of believers have come to light again. The Reformer insisted that the terms "kings and priests" should become as current in the Church as the term "Christians." He therefore explained at length and in all simplicity just what these titles are meant to convey in Holy Writ. We shall make use of much that he has said.

The more we meditate on the titles thus bestowed upon us, the more we find that we must think more highly of ourselves in our connection with the Savior. We are spiritually of royal descent. Actually we are nothing less than kings. It is true, in one sense we are slaves, "bondmen" as the Greek has it, owned in soul and body by our Lord, so that we belong wholly to him as our King, his word and will supreme for us, to be obeyed in all things without question. Yet in another sense we are kings. There is no one above us save Christ and God. Joined to our Lord and made one with him, we do indeed rule and reign with him. And while as yet we are uncrowned, there are heavenly crowns laid up for us and for all that love his appearing. 2 Tim. 4, 8.

In the same way we are truly priests unto God. Christ indeed is our High Priest and as such stands alone in his greatness. There is only one Mediator between God and man, 1 Tim. 2, 5-6, and there can be no other. His sacrifice alone avails for our sins. But now when we come to God by him, our coming makes us also priests unto God. In approaching the throne of grace through our great High Priest we ourselves exercise priestly rights and functions.

It will do us good to think of these things, and thus to rise to the level of our high calling.

St. John speaks of us as kings and priests in three places in Revelation.

He says of Jesus, the faithful witness, the first begotten of the dead, and the prince of the kings of the earth, who loved us and washed us from our sins in his own blood, that he *"hath made us kings and priests unto God and his Father."* Rev. 1, 6.

Again, when the apostle describes the opening of the book with the seven seals, he reports the song that was sung in heaven in praise of the Lamb who was slain and who redeemed us unto God. This song closes with the words: *"And hast made us unto our God kings and priests: and we shall reign on the earth."* Rev. 5, 10.

A third time St. John says of all those who have part in the first resurrection, on whom the second death has no power, *"they shall be priests of God and of Christ, and shall reign with him a thousands years."* Rev. 20, 6.

St. John writes as if there were two separate titles, namely first "kings" and then "priests." Yet a glance shows us that when he states what these kings and priests do, he uses only one verb — they *shall reign.* This is a hint that the two titles really go together and form a unit, even also as he combines them and draws no special line between them.

St. Peter helps us on this point. He turns the title "Kings" into an adjective and connects it with the noun "priests"; "But ye are a chosen generation, *a royal priesthood,* an holy nation, a peculiar people: that ye should shew forth the praises of him who hath called you out of darkness into his marvelous light." 1 Pet. 2, 9. We now see that the two terms express a unit idea. These kings are always priests; these priests always kings. We might call them priestly kings, but the Church is content to follow St. Peter when he writes:

A ROYAL PRIESTHOOD

This is the standard term that has come into constant use.

We must thank this apostle for two additional points.

First, for the synonyms which he places beside the expression "a royal priesthood." They help to show what this priesthood really is. As such we are "a chosen generation," elected by God himself for our high position and function. We are "an holy nation," separated from the world and set apart for God and for divine service. We are in addition "a peculiar people," or more literally "a people for God's own possession," belonging to him in a peculiar manner, intended also for a peculiar work. The better we understand these synonyms, the more will we realize what our priesthood really is and involves.

In the second place St. Peter adds the function for which we have thus been chosen, set apart, and made God's possession as a royal priesthood. It is, to "shew forth the praises of him, who hath called us out of darkness into his marvelous light." This is our distinctive task as royal priests. God has made something of us, and naturally now expects something from us. Our titles are by no means static, they are highly dynamic. By what we are and by all that we can do, at all times and under all circumstances, we are to make God's excellencies shine forth into men's hearts, so that they too may join us and show forth his praises.

A king has no one above him but God. All others are beneath him, else he would be king only in a nominal way. Now that is exactly our spiritual position as Christian believers. There is no one above us save God and Christ alone.

In this respect we are like Christ Jesus himself. He is King indeed. He was that, even in his lowliness, for instance, when he stood before the Roman governor Pilate.

He was governed only and wholly by his **Father's will.**
Only his kingship rested on his Incarnation and redemptive
work, while ours rests on him, on being made one with
him by our regeneration and faith. We did **not make**
him King, but he made us kings.

Now it is exactly the same with our priesthood. A
true priest has direct access to God, without any human
mediation. Else he would not be priest in the full sense
of the word. So every believer has direct access to God
and needs no human mediation.

Here again we are like Christ Jesus. He was a priest,
or to distinguish him from all other priests, he was the
High Priest. With his all-atoning blood he entered the
Holy of Holies in heaven and effected an eternal redemption for us. And now by him we too have the right to
go directly to God. Where once Israel needed human
priests as mediators, we need none. Only Christ's priesthood rests on his Incarnation and redemptive work; ours
rests on him, on our being made one with him by our
new birth and life of faith. Nor did we make him High
Priest; it is he that makes us priests.

It is this unit idea of having no man above us or between
God and us, that lies back of these titles "kings and priests,"
or "a royal priesthood." Let nothing ever lower this our
exalted position. "Ye are bought with a price; be not
the servants of men." 1 Cor. 7, 23.

One thing more should be noted in these titles. They
are always used in the plural "kings" and "priests." St.
Peter's collective "a royal priesthood" has the sense of a
plural. The Bible thus views us not as so many individual
priests and kings. As a royal priest you cannot possibly
stand by yourself. We are one unified body. We meet
the same thought in other titles applied to Christian believers. They form one household, one nation, members
of one living body.

This, for one thing, puts us all on one and the same level. Our earthly relations may differ greatly. One may be a prince, another a pauper; one a millionaire, another a day laborer; one a doctor with many titles of learning, another a school boy or girl. In Christ Jesus we are all alike, all equally kings and priests.

At the same time these plurals combine us on this high level. Our honors, rights, possessions, and obligations are ours conjointly. They literally tie us together. As a believer you cannot be a king without me being one together with you. It is the same with being a priest. This is what is usually expressed by the grand title

UNA SANCTA,

the Latin for the One Holy Christian Church, the Communion of Saints.

Kings and priests — these are our titles, given us by the Lord himself in his Holy Word. By his grace and Spirit think of yourself always as a member in this holy, blessed, and glorious company.

The Title-Bearers

Just as a Christian may be surprised when first he finds himself ranked among kings and priests in the Bible, so also he may at first have his misgivings about assuming the high position thus assigned to him in the Bible. For it is certainly no small thing to be a real king. And equally it is no small thing to be a true priest standing always in the presence of God.

It will not do then to be satisfied with the low requirements some have dared to set for membership in the churches of to-day: 1) a willingness to join; 2) a desire to live a moral life; 3) readiness to pay to the church and to work in her interest. It would be highly extravagant language to call members of this type "kings and priests unto God."

To whom does the Bible accord these precious titles. In a word only to

TRUE BELIEVERS,

but certainly to all of these.

A careful reader of the Bible cannot help but be struck by the great mass of saving truth that is laid down like a grand foundation for the declaration that we are kings and priests unto God. Here are practically all the crown jewels of the Christian faith, blazing in all their heavenly refulgence; and placed in the center is this diamond of purest water, our royal priesthood. Only as we look at the grandness and the splendor of the setting can we fully appreciate the value of the glorious central piece.

Take St. John's first statement, Rev. 1, 4-6: "Grace be unto you and peace, from him which is, and which was, and which is to come; and from the seven Spirits which are before his throne; and from Jesus Christ, who is the faithful witness, and the first begotten of the dead, and the prince of the kings of the earth. Unto him that loved us, and washed us from our sins in his own blood, and hath made us *kings and priests* unto God and his Father; to him the glory and dominion for ever and ever. Amen."

Beyond question here is voiced a grand summary of the Christian faith. These words speak

1) Of the Holy Trinity.

2) Of the God-man Jesus Christ.

3) Of his eternity: which was, and is, and is to come.

4) Of the witness of his atoning death, 1 Tim. 6, 13.

5) Of his resurrection as the first begotten of the dead.

6) Of his lordship over all the kings of the earth.

7) Of his wonderful love and grace.

8) Of the washing from sins in his expiating blood, which means justification, pardon, and cleansing before God.

9) Of the peace with God that follows grace and pardon.

10) Of the glory and dominion that is God's for ever.

Only in the light of these divine realities and in fullest connection with them all can we understand what it means that Jesus has made us "kings and priests unto God." And it becomes very plain that only they are such kings and priests who receive these great truths in their hearts. In other words, these kings and priests are true believers.

St. John's second statement is briefer, Rev. 5, 9-10: "And they sung a new song, saying, Thou art worthy to take the book, and to open the seals thereof: for thou was slain, and hast redeemed us to God by thy blood out of every kindred, and tongue, and people, and nation; and hast made us unto our God *kings and priests*: and we shall reign on the earth."

This is the song that resounded in heaven when the Lamb took the book with the seven seals that no one but he could open. This song speaks

1) Of the Lamb himself in heaven, the Son of God and Son of man.

2) Of the slaying of the Lamb in sacrifice for our sin and guilt.

3) Of the sufficiency of his sacrifice, since the Lamb is now exalted in heaven.

4) Of the mighty effect of his death, namely redemption to God by his blood.

5) Of the extent of that redemption, winning a Church from all kindreds, tongues, people, and nations.

Here St. John points to the very center of the Christian faith, namely the redemption wrought by the Lamb's sacrifice, as the basis for our kingship and priesthood as believers. The personal way in which this is put: "redeemed *us*," just as in St. John's first passage, makes it very plain once more that only true believers, who have embraced this redemption and clasped to their hearts its grace and gifts, can be counted among the kings and priests of God who shall reign on the earth.

We may repeat this observation in Rev. 20, 6: "Blessed and holy is he that hath part in the first resurrection: on such the second death hath no power, but they shall be *priests* of God and of Christ, and *shall reign* with him a thousand years."

The ground on which our priesthood and kingship rest is here described as

1) The first resurrection, namely the transfer of the soul into the blessed life of heaven. Some think this resurrection signifies conversion, but the word "resurrection" is here used symbolically. The second resurrection would thus be the transfer of the body into heaven.

2) The escape from the power of the second death. Believers must still suffer the first death, which is the

separation of soul and body. They are forever delivered
from the second death, which is the separation of both
soul and body from the eternal source of life and light
in God. The second death is the fire of hell, Rev. 20,
14-15.

3) The blessedness and holiness that go with this
resurrection and deliverance from death. It is a wondrous
happy state, basking in the full light of grace: It is also
a holy state, receiving the cleansing from sin day by day
in true repentance and faith.

Yes, they who possess what is here described are priests
of God and of Christ, royal priests, who shall reign with
him a thousand years, namely all through the New Testament era, which begins with the Incarnation and closes
with the Final Judgment. We commonly call this blessed
and holy company Christ's believers.

St. Peter agrees with St. John in setting the royal priesthood on the solid foundation of the saving realities in
Christ Jesus. In 1 Pet. 2, 4 etc. he describes at length

1) The Great Corner Stone Christ Jesus laid in Sion,
a precious Stone for all believers, but a Stone of stumbling
and a Rock of offense for all who are disobedient in
unbelief.

2) The apostle adds our election, verse 9, our holiness, our belonging to God as his peculiar possession.

Again we see, it is the heart of the Gospel which makes
us " a royal priesthood." None of the disobedient can
belong to it, only they who obey in faith, and by faith
receive into their hearts the divine realities of Salvation.

Now comes St. Paul and helps us to take the final step
in determining who the bearers of the great titles "kings
and priests unto God" really are. Where the other two
apostles used only the pronoun *"us"* in naming the believers, this apostle goes more into detail.

Gal. 3, 26-29: "Ye are all the children of God by faith
in Christ Jesus. For as many of you as have been bap-

tized into Christ have put on Christ. There is neither Jew nor Greek, there is neither bond nor free, there is neither male nor female: for ye are all one in Christ Jesus. And if ye be Christ's, then are ye Abraham's seed, and heirs according to the promise."

The kings and priests who are God's peculiar possession, St. Paul calls "the children of God," Abraham's seed, and heirs according to the promise. But he adds this illuminating statement, that in this great body of believers no distinctions count, whether of race, of social and civil position, or of sex. Behold thus

THE CHURCH UNIVERSAL,

called also in the language of the Apostles' Creed "the Holy Catholic Church." "Catholic" simply means universal, all-embracing.

In St. Paul's days a religious gulf separated Jews and Greeks. Only as one was a Jew by birth, or became a convert to Judaism, could he be counted as belonging to Abraham's seed, or God's children. In the Christian Church this gulf has vanished. Jew and Greek are admitted on identical terms into the Communion of Saints.

In the old world there was also the mighty difference between free men and slaves. Recall St. Paul's lovely epistle to Philemon on behalf of the slave Onesimus, who had run away from his master, whom St. Paul had converted, and who was now returning to his master — still a slave, but spiritually equal with his Christian master. In the Church master and slave sit side by side, both being one in Christ Jesus.

The oriental world still makes a deplorable difference between male and female. Even in the synagogues of the orthodox Jews women are shut in behind screens. Mohammedanism made woman the slave of man and debates whether she has an immortal soul. In the East there are still three burden-bearers, the camel, the ass, and woman.

All this is wiped out in the Church. The spiritual rights of both sexes are equal.

We must be careful not to read St. Paul's statement concerning Jew and Greek, bond and free, male and female as pertaining only to adults. Often this is done unwittingly. His words include the children, down to the tiniest babe. Jews and Greeks are such from infancy on. Already by birth a babe is either free or a slave. The apostle was careful not to write: "neither man nor woman," which would have meant adults. He wrote: "neither male nor female." Sex extends to every infant.

So our little ones too may be "the children of God" and as God's own possession assume their place in the royal priesthood.

The great thing that counts in the Church is

CHRISTIAN BAPTISM,

namely "the washing of regeneration and renewing of the Holy Ghost," Tit. 3, 5; the new birth of water and the Spirit, John 3, 5.

Why does Baptism count so decisively? Because by Baptism we "put on Christ," which means that the filthy garment of our sin is removed (Acts 22, 16), and we are clothed in the wedding garment (Matth. 22, 11-12) of Christ's righteousness (Is. 61, 10). Every soul (Acts 2, 41) sanctified and cleansed with the washing of water by the Word (Eph. 5, 26), which is Baptism, is joined to Christ. All who are thus joined to him are "one in Christ Jesus" (Gal. 3, 28) and constitute the chosen generation, the holy nation, the peculiar people who form the royal priesthood.

Not that there is anything mechanical or magical about Baptism. Whoever loses what the Sacrament gave him might as well never have been baptized. Whoever receives the Sacrament hypocritically never gets what it would give to him.

So it is quite the same to say: the royal priesthood includes all believers; and: the royal priesthood includes all who by Baptism have put on Christ Jesus. There are no limitations of nationality, color, civil position, sex, age, or other human differences. While there are such natural differences among the kings and priests of God, these differences in no way interfere with their kingship and priesthood. All natural differences are sanctified and blessed by grace, and are thus made subservient to the royal priesthood which rises above them.

It will not be difficult now to answer the question concerning the faulty and erring believers.

Every man, woman, or child inwardly joined to Christ belongs to the royal priesthood as long as that inward tie holds. That tie, however, may be strong, or it may be weak. Littleness of faith makes the tie weak, so also a faith mixed up with convictions contrary to the realities of the Word. A thread may still hold a soul to Christ; a cable is much stronger. Many have fallen out of the royal priesthood because the tie that held them grew weak to the breaking point.

Again, to lose any part of the saving truth in Christ Jesus, or to substitute for that truth empty human notions, must prove a great hindrance to the exercise of our calling as a royal priesthood. To think in a wrong way about our Savior, about any part of his work or his teaching, to that extent prevents us from serving him as we should in our office of kings and priests. Besetting sins and all errors in living the Christian life act in the same manner. No wonder the apostles pray so fervently and constantly that we may grow in knowledge (Eph. 1, 16 etc.) and in grace (2 Pet. 3, 18), until we reach the full maturity of faith, the full stature of manhood in Christ Jesus (Eph. 4, 13-14).

The kings and priests of God should be fully fitted for their high and holy station.

The Royal Reign and Priestly Sacrifice

One of the surprising things in the Bible is the way Christ's kingship is connected with his priesthood, his royalty with his suffering, his power with his death.

What Psalm 110 foretold concerning David's son and David's Lord has come true in the highest degree. Look at verse 4 of that Psalm: "The Lord hath sworn, and will not repent, Thou art a priest for ever after the order of Melchizedek." Then compare at length the seventh chapter of Hebrews. In the entire Old Testament only Melchizedek appears as king and priest in one person. There were many kings and also many priests, but always separate persons. Even David and Solomon were only kings not priests. Even Aaron was only a high priest, not a king. Melchizedek was both king of Salem and priest of the Most High God. In a remarkable way he thus prefigured Christ as

KING AND HIGH PRIEST IN ONE PERSON.

Our redemption rests on this combination or union. Look at Jesus before Pilate — he wears a crown of thorns, a purple robe, and carries a scepter rod. To the governor's question, "Art thou a king then?" he replies that he is, not indeed over a kingdom of this world, but a far higher king. Remember that this our King was at that very moment making himself a sacrifice for our sins and thus doing his High Priestly work.

On the cross the malefactor addresses our dying High Priest as a King, "Lord, remember me when thou comest into thy kingdom."

In the superscription on the cross Pilate pronounces
Jesus a king in three different languages. And when Jesus
dies the centurion under the cross recognizes the divine
Kingship of our High Priest and declares, "Truly this
was the Son of God."

We may sum it up: the King of kings alone could be
our Great High Priest. It required a royal sacrifice to
expiate our sins. And again: that this Great King might
be for us the Prince of Life and the Prince of Peace,
he had to be also our Great High Priest and lay down
his life for our ransom.

Only the Lamb can be our King. The Lamb that was
slain sits on the royal throne in heaven, and from that
throne makes High Priestly intercession for us. When
St. John beheld him in his glory he heard these words
from his lips, "I am he that liveth and was dead" (High
Priest and sacrifice); "and behold I live for ever, Amen,
and have the keys of hell and of death" (King eternal),
Rev. 1, 18.

Thus in Christ kingship and priesthood are indissolubly
welded together. We may speak of them separately, as
also we often do; but we understand them best when we
note how they are joined together.

We Christians are patterned after Christ. As he was
King and High Priest in one person, with his kingship
and priesthood joined together, so we now are kings and
priests unto God, and our kingship and priesthood are
joined in a royal priesthood.

With startling positiveness the Bible declares that we
Christians "reign with Christ." There is Rev. 5, 10,
"And we shall reign on the earth." Again Rev. 20, 6,
"And shall reign with him a thousand years." The place
as well as the era of our reign is thus declared.

But actually, as we live here on earth there does not
seem to be anything royal about us at all. Compared
with the regal splendor of earthly kings and potentates

we are certainly a humble company. Most of us are just ordinary working people. We live and die with only a few friends and a little earthly property. It would excite the worst ridicule of many an unbeliever to hear people like this claiming royalty and power to reign as kings.

Yet the fact remains — we are royal. Christ has lifted us so high that this predicate alone is sufficient to describe our exalted position. In his famous essay "On the Liberty of a Christian" Luther put it into these unforgetable words, "A Christian is a free lord over all things, and subject to no one." He proved it at length, and the Christian world to this day cannot forget his words.

OUR ROYAL REIGN WITH CHRIST.

What is there so royal about us Christians, and how do we reign?

First of all, there is

Our Royal Birth.

God is King. We are his children. That makes us royal. Christ is King. He calls us his brethren. That again makes us royal.

Distinguish between the kingship of God over all creatures, the inanimate as well as the animate, and his kingship over the Church. The creature world is merely **subject** to God, and does not share in his royal powers. But by our new birth we Christians have entered the spiritual world. We are lifted into *union with God*. The Triune God dwells in us. Christ is in us, and we in him. The Son has made us free, and we are free indeed. John 8, 36. We are made partakers of the divine nature. 2 Pet. 1, 4. In this sense we are spiritually kings, of royal descent and birth, possessing royal prerogatives and powers.

This royalty differs completely from the dominion over the lower creature world originally given to man in creation. Sin has marred this dominion so that now it is only partial. Man yields eventually to the forces of nature, and his body succumbs in death. The real difference between man's dominion and the Christian's royal reign is that the former consists merely of superior *brain* power and works in the world of nature, while the latter consists of a new *soul* power and works in both the world of nature and of the spirit.

In the second place, there is

Our Royal Power.

This is the spiritual and eternal power of the Word of God. The moment we are reborn by the Word of God (1 Pet. 1, 23) that Word abides in us (1 John 3, 9) and becomes our possession. We are to be filled with it (Col. 3, 16), to live by it, to know all its power, and ourselves also to use that power.

Need we describe the power of this Word? It is the sword of the Spirit, Eph. 6, 17. Remember a king's scepter must always be backed by his sword. It is quick and powerful, dividing even soul and spirit, Heb. 4, 12. It pulls down strongholds, casts down imaginations and every high thing that exalteth itself against the knowledge of God, and brings into captivity every thought to the obedience of Christ, 2 Cor. 10, 4-5. As the Gospel this Word is the power of God unto salvation, Rom. 1, 16. When preached it seems foolishness to the wise, but is none the less God's power to save, 1 Cor. 1, 18. It outlasts both heaven and earth, Matth. 24, 35, and not one jot or tittle (one letter or part of a letter) shall remain unfulfilled, Math. 5, 18. And Jesus himself gives us this mighty Word with all its power, John 17, 5 and 14.

To possess this Word and power is to be spiritually *a king* indeed, and to use this power is *to reign* on earth.

When the humblest Christian pronounces a Word of God his pronouncement will stand. Men may bring all the forces at their command against it, all will be in vain —that humble Christian is bound to prevail. If he condemns unbelief, falsehood, folly, and wickedness, and the men who adhere to these, that condemnation stands, a royal decree that no human rage can annul. "He that is spiritual judgeth all things, yet he himself is judged of no man." 1 Cor. 2, 15. The saints shall judge the world, 1 Cor. 6, 2, even angels themselves, verse 3. Likewise when a Christian, be he ever so slowly, commends repentance, faith, the truth of God, and the virtues and good works of faith, and the men who accept these, that commendation will stand, again a royal decree that no human denial and ridicule can possibly annul. We reign with Christ when thus we use his Word.

In the third place,

Our Royal Servants

show that we are kings and reign as such.

St. Paul declares 1 Cor. 3, 21-23, "All things are yours, whether Paul or Apollos, or Cephas, or the world, or life, or death, or things present, or things to come; all are yours; and ye are Christ's and Christ is God's." Did ever any earthly king have such an array of servants? Again, Rom. 8, 29, "He that spared not his own Son, but delivered him up for us all, how shall he not with him also freely give us all things?" With all things as our servants, our royalty is beyond question.

Here is the service we receive from these countless servants of ours, "We know that all things work together for good to them that love God," etc., Rom. 8, 28. Each,

in its own way, according to its capacity and nature, does
us some "good," brings us some benefit or advantage.
It is as if this multitude of servants surrounded us and
on bended knees held out their precious offerings to us.
Some of these servants, like pain, loss, injury, sickness,
grief, and death, may at first have a strange look to us
who do not know our own royalty sufficiently.   It is
God who commissions them all and makes each one bring
us some blessing, so that as kings unto God we shall
lack nothing.

The highest of these servants are the angels.   It ought
to give us a new and a truer conception of our exalted
position as kings that reign with Christ, to learn that
God's angels stoop down to serve us.   "Are they not
ministering spirits, sent forth to minister for them who
shall be heirs of salvation?" Heb. 1, 14.   Our high position is indicated by the expression "heirs of salvation."
That this includes even our little children Jesus himself
indicates when he tells us, "Their angels do always behold
the face of my Father which is in heaven." Matth. 18,
10.   We can especially rely on their protection in danger,
for "the angel of the Lord encampeth round about them
that fear him and delivereth them," Ps. 34, 7.   No earthly
king ever had servitors so high and so mighty.

In the fourth place,

Our Royal Victories

prove that we are truly kings.

In our royal priesthood we have many enemies, all
seeking our spiritual destruction, but we triumph over
them all.   All we need do is to resist the devil, and he
flees from us, James 4, 7.   Born of God we overcome the
world; in fact, our faith is the victory that overcometh
the world, John 5, 4.   Our own sinful members we mortify,

Col. 3, 5, and the flesh with the affections and lusts we crucify, Gal. 5, 24. And thus we join in St. Paul's victory song. "I am persuaded that neither death, nor life, nor angels, nor principalities, nor powers, nor things present, nor things to come, nor height, nor depth, nor any other creature, shall be able to separate us from the love of God, which is in Christ Jesus our Lord." Rom. 8, 38-39.

We are thus kings indeed, but during this life we are and remain *uncrowned kings,* waiting for our crowns. St. Paul looked forward to the crown that was laid up for him, 2 Tim. 4, 8. St. James calls the man blessed who endures temptation, for he shall receive the promised crown of life from the Lord, James 1, 12. St. Peter tells the pastors who do their work well that they shall receive from the Chief Shepherd a crown of glory that fadeth not away, 1 Pet. 5, 4. And Christ himself through St. John promises all who are faithful unto death the crown of life, Rev. 2, 10; 3, 11. What a wondrous coronation day that will be when the entire royalty of believers will be assembled before the throne of the King of kings to receive their heavenly crowns at his hands! To one he will say, "Have thou authority over ten cities!" and to another, "Be thou also over five cities!" And we shall sit with him in his throne (Rev. 3, 21) and reign with him (2 Tim. 2, 12) for ever.

In our waiting to be crowned we are like Christ during the days of his lowliness. He was a King as he lay in the manger and as he hung on the cross, an uncrowned King. But in due time God glorified him (John 17, 1) and crowned him with glory and honor (Heb. 2, 9) at his own right hand. So now we too wait, and the day of our coronation is not far off.

Our royal birth entitles us to reign.

Our royal power enables us to reign, and by it we do reign.

Our royal servants show that we are worthy before God to reign.

Our royal victories glorify our reign.

But from our royal birth on till our last royal victory, which is the victory over death, our reign is "with Christ" alone. By his grace and gifts he is ours, and by our faith we are his. Thus we share in his royal position and reign. The moment we lose him all our royalty is gone.

OUR PRIESTLY SACRIFICE THROUGH CHRIST.

What is there priestly about us Christians? And what priestly sacrifices do we bring?

First of all

Our Priestly Anointing.

It is Luther who again and again emphasizes and explains that in our Baptism we are anointed by the Holy Spirit, and by that anointing are truly made priests unto God. The very name "Christian" means "one who is anointed," and thus one who is a spiritual priest.

Luther bases this on the Bible doctrine of Baptism. For Jesus calls Baptism the new birth of water and the Spirit, John 3, 5; and St. Paul says it is the washing of regeneration and renewing of the Holy Ghost, Tit. 3, 5. Thus it is Baptism through which we receive the "unction from the Holy Ghost," 1 John 2, 20; "and the anointing which ye have received of him abideth in you," verse 27.

"God has anointed us," 2 Cor. 1, 21, and that makes us priests.

Looked at in another way our Baptism and new birth make us one with Christ, our anointed High Priest. This union with him as Priest gives us priestly character likewise. Luther, for this reason, calls us "genuine priest-children," who inherit their very name "Christians" from "Christ" through Baptism and the faith that goes with it. Luther says that even St. Peter became a priest only in the same way as you and I, namely by believing the Gospel.

Therefore Luther wants the name "priests" for us made as current and common as are the names "Christians" and "children of God." For we all have in common one Baptism and Gospel, one grace and inheritance of heaven, one Holy Spirit and one God the Father and Lord Christ; and are all one in him. He a Priest and we priests through him.

Our priestly anointing produced by Baptism and faith goes together with

Our Priestly Purification.

Beyond question a true priest must be purified. As a priest he is to come into the holy presence of God. How dare he do it with an unholy heart or with unholy hands? Even of Christ it is said, "Such a High Priest became us, who is holy, harmless, undefiled, separate from sinners." Heb. 7, 26. Also the sacrifice he brought was without spot or blemish.

It is Christ himself who purifies us as priests unto God and thus makes us fit to stand in his holy presence.

"Christ loved the Church and gave himself for it, that he might sanctify and cleanse it with the washing of water by the Word (Baptism), that he might present it to himself a glorious Church, not having spot or wrinkle or any such thing, but that it should be holy and without blemish." Eph. 5, 25-27.

This is the cleansing that washes away all the stains and spots of sin, that justifies before God and pardons, that clothes us in "the robe of righteousness" (Is. 61, 10; 1 Cor. 1, 30; 2 Cor. 5, 21), so that with boldness we may approach the throne of grace (Heb. 4, 16).

"Having therefore boldness to enter into the holiest by the blood of Jesus, . . . let us draw near with a true heart in full assurance of faith, having our hearts sprinkled from an evil conscience and our bodies washed with pure water." Heb. 10, 19 and 22. To draw near and enter the holiest is to act as a priest in God's presence. Only he may do this who is sprinkled and washed by the cleansing of Baptism.

Lest there be any misunderstanding let us emphasize the chief point. It is the priestly purification which Christ gives us that makes us priests and fits us to stand before God. It is not the holiness of heart and life to which we attain. Only the former is perfect, the latter always has flaws.

Anointed and purified we are ready to bring unto God

Our Priestly Sacrifice.

When Luther describes our work as priests he makes three parts, to teach, to sacrifice, to pray. Really there is only one part, namely to sacrifice. Teaching and praying, and whatever else may be added, are all included in this one.

Only one who sacrifices deserves the name "priest." If one fails to sacrifice he is actually not a priest.

This is true of Christ. He sacrificed himself for us — that made him a priest. It is true even in false and erring religions. In some way they have sacrifices, and they who perform them are for this reason called priests. So our priestly function is to sacrifice.

There are two kinds of sacrifice, the bloody and the bloodless, the sinoffering and the thankoffering. The one is brought *for* the *guilty* sinner; the other *by* the *pardoned* sinner. We are able to bring only the latter unto God.

These two kinds of sacrifice were used in the Old Testament, according to detailed arrangements made by God himself. In the New Testament there is only one bloody sacrifice for sin, that of Christ on the cross for the sins of the world. The effect of this is eternal, Heb. 9, 12. We are to render the bloodless sacrifices, which in the New Testament are all spiritual.

No sacrifice of ours can possibly remove sin.

"Should my tears forever flow,
Should my zeal no languor know,
This for sin could not atone;
Thou must save, and Thou alone."

In fact, no man in his sins dares approach the throne of God as a priest. Only when our sin is removed by Christ's sacrifice may we offer sacrifice on our part. In fact, then we cannot help but "offer up spiritual sacrifices, acceptable to God by Jesus Christ." 1 Pet. 2, 5.

What are these *spiritual and acceptable sacrifices?* We might give different lists, all quite satisfactory, as also others have done. For our purpose it will be well to follow St. Paul.

"Present *your bodies* a living sacrifice, holy, acceptable unto God, which is your reasonable service." Rom. 12, 1.

"And *your members* as instruments of righteousness unto God." Rom. 6, 13. "As ye have yielded your members servants to uncleanness and to iniquity unto iniquity; even so now yield *your members* servants to righteousness unto holiness." Rom. 6, 19. St. Paul is comprehensive. This is the entire sacrifice we are to make.

It is well to note that as Christ was Priest and Lamb (a bloody sacrifice) in one person, so we too are to be priests and the sacrifice (bloodless and living in our case) in one person. We, the priests, are to lay ourselves, the sacrifice, on the altar of God as a thankoffering.

We likewise observe that in bringing the body and bodily members as a sacrifice to God the soul and mind are invariably involved. Only a mind transformed and renewed (Rom. 12, 2) is able to offer the body unto God. "Be ye renewed in the spirit of your mind." Eph. 4, 23. St. Paul is able to call the body and its members the sacrifice, because the body is the instrument through which the soul works in this earthly life.

Luther made a strange slip when in commenting on 1 Pet. 2, 5 he considered the body we are to bring as the sacrifice our old Adam. He puts it thus: "what of the old Adam we have"; and in his drastic way called it "the lazy old ass." No; God accepts no lazy old ass as an offering. Take the old carcass out and bury it! Not our sinful nature or our sinful members are fit to be brought as a sacrifice to God, only our sanctified nature and our sanctified members; not the old Adam, but the new man in Christ Jesus.

Let us name some of these members.

Our *hearts* are to be filled with the Word of God. This means contrition, a crushing of the heart under the sense of sin wrought by the Word. "The sacrifices of God are a broken spirit: a broken and a contrite heart, O God, thou wilt not despise." Ps. 51, 17. It means also a sure and joyful trust wrought by the Gospel promises of the Word. Our faith and its confession are "the sacrifices of righteousness" twice mentioned in the Psalms (4, 5; 51, 19), called "an offering in righteousness" in Mal. 3, 3. And we must add for the heart the willing obedience of love which follows every prompting of the Word. Jesus himself makes it the test of love that we "keep his commandments," his "words," and his "sayings," John 14, 21 and 23-24, namely his Gospel behests. Thus will we be "obedient children," 1 Pet. 1, 14-15, furnishing the proof "whether ye be obedient in all things," 2 Cor. 2, 9.

Since the heart, in Scripture language, is the central organ of the soul or spirit, governing all our thinking, feeling, and willing, to sacrifice the heart unto God really includes all other sacrifice, the offering to God of our whole being.

Our *ears* are to hear the Word of God, and like gateways to let that Word go down into our hearts. We are to rejoice in hearing every good thing, and to grieve when we hear evil.

Our *eyes* are to look up to God, behold his wonderful works, read his Word, see with delight all that is good, behold with sorrow the evil.

Our *lips* are to speak the Word, and in all their speaking be controlled by the Word. Our conversation is to be pure, edifying to the hearer, in favor of all that is good, against everything wrong and base. This is the priestly "teaching" that Luther emphasizes. Petitions, requests, thanksgiving, praise, and intercession are to rise to our lips. This is the priestly "praying" which Luther makes prominent. Hosea 14, 2 calls it "the calves of our lips."

Our *feet* are to run the way of God's commandments, Ps. 119, 32, to walk in the paths of righteousness, Ps. 23, 3, quick to perform the Lord's errands, ever avoiding the company and assembly of the ungodly, Ps. 1, 1.

Our *hands* are to fold in prayer. They are to bring willing offerings of our substance to God, for the work of his Church and for alms and charity. They are to perform countless deeds of love, kindness, and all Christian virtues, for the benefit of men and for the glory of God.

When sickness and suffering prostrate our body the special opportunity comes to us to offer the sacrifice of humble submission to the will of God, of patient endurance in affliction, and of full reliance on his Word for comfort and strength constantly clinging to him in trustful prayer.

There are still higher levels to which God lifts us in sacrificing ourselves unto him. In this wicked world we

must suffer when we boldly confess his Word and refuse
to deny some part, or even all of it, at the behest of men.
That may mean the loss of position, of the good-will and
favor of men, of income and money, of a good name, of
honor that we might have had, and of other advantages.
To lose these things for Christ's sake is to bring to him
some of the highest sacrifices of which we are capable.
They are priests indeed who rejoice to lay such offerings
at the Savior's feet.

The Bible speaks of these sacrifices in the highest terms,
linking them with Christ's own sufferings. St. Paul calls
them "the fellowship of his sufferings," namely Christ's,
Phil. 3, 10. He says, such sufferings "fill up that which
is behind of the afflictions of Christ," Col. 1, 24. He even
describes the Christians who suffer thus for Christ's sake
as "always bearing about in the body the dying of the
Lord Jesus, that the life also of Jesus might be made
manifest in our body," 2 Cor. 4, 10.

The crown of this sacrifice is martyrdom for Christ and
the Word of his testimony. Stephen was the first who
brought the sacrifice of his life for his Lord. The Lord
himself stood forth to receive his soul. The rage of Saul
added others whose names are known only in heaven.
Herod slew James the brother of John with the sword.
Acts 12, 2. Read Heb. 11, 35 etc. "And I saw the souls
of them that were beheaded for the witness of Jesus, and
for the Word of God, and which had not worshipped the
beast, neither his image, neither had received his mark
upon their foreheads, or in their hands; and they lived
and reigned with Christ a thousand years." Rev. 20, 4.

Thus all through our lives in ever varying ways by means
of our bodies, sometimes even by bodily suffering and
death, we are to "show forth the praises of him who hath
called you out of darkness into his marvelous light,"
1 Pet. 2, 9. His "praises" are his virtues and
excellecies, all that renders him great and blessed to

us who know what he has done for us. There is no higher function of which we are capable in this earthly life than to glorify God in our mortal flesh (or bodies), 2 Cor. 4, 11. To render this acceptable sacrifice of ourselves unto God makes us indeed a royal priesthood, and we shall stand forever in the presence of our God.

Priests and Pastors

What is the relation of the royal priesthood of believers to the office of the holy ministry?

Luther already faced this question and gave it the correct answer.

When he began the work of Reformation the members of the church had been robbed of their royal priesthood. In addition they were placed in complete subjection to a spurious hierarchical order of priests at whose head stood the pope. There was thus a double perversion fatally interlocked. The genuine priesthood, spiritual in its nature, had been cancelled and lost; and over the church thus degraded. there was reared a false ecclesiastical order of priests without warrant from the Lord.

By means of the Bible Luther regained for the church the spiritual priesthood of her members and also true evangelical pastors instead of ecclesiastical priests.

Almost immediately a new perversion arose. Fanatical sects began to abuse Luther's own teaching on the universal priesthood of believers. Because the Word of God is given to all believers alike as kings and priests, these fanatics, generally known as *Schwaermer,* concluded that no further authority was needed for any man who felt the impulse thereto, to preach and teach publicly. They denied that one must have a call from a Christian congregation before assuming the work that belongs to the pastors in the Church. The result was all manner of confusion and grave abuses where these ideas prevailed during Reformation times.

In a later age the so-called Pietists were affected by the same error. They laid a morbid stress on piety and holiness. The organized work of Christian congregations un-

der properly called pastors was largely despised. Those
who were convinced of their own holiness met in so-called
"conventicles," exclusive gatherings where they expounded
the Word in their own fashion and prayed in a way they
deemed truly spiritual. They imagined their universal
priesthood was enough, and had little use for pastors,
except such as fell in with their supposedly "spiritual"
ways.

The extreme in this respect is reached by the Quakers,
and others like them, who have abolished the office of the
ministry entirely in their midst, and depend upon the Spirit
to move individual members to speak in their meetings.

A variety of other wrong ideas has appeared from time
to time regarding the priesthood of believers and the
ministry, persisting even to the present. Either the ministry is unduly elevated and made too independent of
the congregations, or its rights and powers are confounded
with those of the universal priesthood and robbed of their
distinctiveness.

For us to exercise properly the royal priesthood which
Christ has bestowed upon the members of his Church,
we must know, first of all, the difference between this
priesthood and the holy ministry, and secondly, the real
relation of these two to each other.

The difference may be put into two words:

PRIVATE — PUBLIC.

The universal priesthood is exercised only in a private
way. The pastoral office in Christian congregations is
exercised only in a public way.

To make this difference still clearer we may add the
point on which it really turns. This is the congregational
call. He who has this call is a pastor, and the work he
does by authority of this call is for that very reason

termed public. All others in the Church, who have no such call, are not pastors; and the work done on the strength only of the universal priesthood is for this very reason termed private. Thus it is

THE CALL

that distinguishes between priests and pastors.

A few illustrations may aid us.

A Christian family assembles for family worship — as indeed all Christian families ought to do. It may be a large family, with a goodly number of children, some servants, and perhaps several visitors. The father as the head of the family conducts the worship. Let us say that he reads from the Bible and offers a prayer, one from a devotional book, or one freely spoken by himself. He is acting as a royal priest. So are all those engaged in the worship with him, down to the little children. Because the royal priesthood is wholly sufficient for what the father does in this service, as well as for what the others do, therefore the entire proceeding is private. It is all just between the Lord and that father and his family. There is no congregational call, and nothing is done in compliance with such a call.

One of the members of the Church is seriously ill. Let us say, it is a child. The mother kneels at the bedside and pours out her heart in prayer to God. Let us say it is an older person. A few anxious friends come in. Before they leave one of them reads a few verses from the Bible and adds a short prayer. Here again the worship is private. All the rights used are those of the universal priesthood, none of them those of the pastoral call.

A couple of families in the same town find no church of their own that they can reach. They meet on Sunday in one of the homes and arrange a little Sunday School, perhaps with the children in one class, and the grown people in another. When Sunday School is ended they have a short service. One of the men reads the liturgy, announces the hymns, and reads the sermon for the day from some good sermon book. What is this but a beautiful exercise of the royal priesthood? Yet it is all properly termed private, for no pastoral call is involved.

Would that we had more of this blessed exercise of the universal priesthood among our members! We have pictured only a few samples; there are many more that could be sketched. The last example should be especially noted. It shows how many a mission might be started, with a mission pastor finally taking charge — in each town a precious nucleus with power like a seed to grow indefinitely.

But here is a pastor busy with the labors laid upon him by the call from his congregation. He visits the sick, reads the Scriptures to them, adds perhaps a few words of helpful explanation, and ends with a prayer. In itself it may all be very much like the ministration of one of his own members for one that is sick. Yet there is a difference. The pastor's act is public, because it is performed under the obligation of his call from the congregation. There may be present only the sick person and the attendant, and even the attendant may remain in another room, leaving the pastor and the patient altogether alone. The pastor's act is official, a part of his call, and thus public.

There is little difficulty in perceiving this when the pastor leads his Sunday School, conducts the services of the congregation and preaches from the pulpit. We all know that he does these things because the congregation has called him to do them. He acts as their representative, by virtue of the authority they have conferred upon him.

Thus it is the call that makes the difference between the universal priesthood and the Christian ministry.

Now let us look at *the relation of the two to each other.*

In giving the Word of God to the members of the Church the Lord has a double purpose.

First of all, he wants each of us to use that Word privately for the spiritual benefit of himself and others. This is our royal and priestly prerogative. Each of us, without distinction of age or sex, is freely to go to the Lord in his Word and there take directly from his own hand for himself and for others all the treasures of the Lord's grace. No one dare thrust himself between us and the Lord in this use of the Word. No one dare force us to come to him first, to receive from him what the Lord would give us or what the Lord would ask of us. Any attempt of this kind is an attempt to take from us our priestly rights before God.

In the second place, the Lord wants his Word proclaimed and applied publicly. As a royal priesthood we are to assemble for united public worship. The apostles themselves have shown us how this is to be done. The Word is to be read, taught and preached in public to us all. Our response is to be one of praise, confession, prayer, and offerings, thus showing in every way our gratitude for that Word and our appreciation of its blessings. Every locality where this public worship is established is thus to become a spiritual center from which the Word with its blessings radiates and reaches out into the community to win others unto faith in Christ. And from these centers messengers of the Word are to be sent out to other localities, near and far away, to plant the Gospel there and found new Christian congregations. In this too the apostles have shown us the way.

When thus we see the members of the royal priesthood gathered together in all the different localities in

CHRISTIAN CONGREGATIONS,

we are on the way to understand how the royal priesthood and the Christian ministry are related to each other.

Only by acting conjointly, by banding together in congregations, are we, the members of the Church, able to maintain public worship and the preaching of the Word. This public use of the Word, and all that goes with it, is ours, not as so many separate priests of God, but in the very nature of the case as collective bodies, each group alike part of the royal priesthood.

In Matth. 28, 19-20 the Lord bids us make disciples of all nations by means of Baptism and the teaching of his Word. In Mark 16, 15-16 he tells us to preach the Gospel to every creature, and promises that all who believe and are baptized shall be saved.

Did he mean that we should do this individually? Am I to go and win a soul here and there, and you likewise — each of us standing and working by himself, and each of the souls we win in turn standing and working alone? We have our answer on the day of Pentecost. On that day 3,000 souls were converted and baptized, and at once they formed one body, a Christian congregation, the mother church of Christendom. All the members held together in close fellowship. And in their midst the doctrine of the apostles was preached, the Sacraments were administered, and there was public worship. Acts 2, 42 etc.

And it was by this public use of the Word that this first congregation grew in a most remarkable way. Starting with 3,000 souls, soon there were 5,000 men, not counting the women and children, Acts 4, 4. A little later there were so many that Luke attempts no count, but simply reports how "multitudes both of men and women" were added, Acts 5, 14, and even "a great company of the (Jewish) priests were obedient to the faith," Acts 6, 7.

And this is the story all through the days of the apostles. Everywhere the believers gathered together and formed congregations. There was one at Rome, at Corinth, a number in Galatia, one in Ephesus, in Philippi, in Colossae, etc. We cannot mention them all here. The Lord himself sent brief letters to seven of them located in Asia Minor, Rev. 2 etc.

Now the one outstanding feature of all of them is that they assemble about the public preaching of the Word in public worship. What the first congregation in Jerusalem did all the rest did likewise. We see it in the history that Luke has left us in the Acts, and in all the letters the apostles wrote to these congregations, in particular also in the letters St. Paul wrote to the two pastors Timothy and Titus.

While there is no specific command in the New Testament that believers are to form congregations, there is overwhelming evidence that this is indeed the Lord's will.

A congregation is a company of believers joined together for maintaining public preaching and worship in their midst. In other words, it is the royal priesthood in any one place jointly providing for the public use of the Word committed unto them by the Lord. We need not trouble about hypocrites. They pretend to be believers, while at heart they are not. They do not belong to the royal priesthood at all. Attached to a congregation, they belong to it only outwardly. They resemble the barnacles on a ship, or the weeds in a wheat field.

This suffices for congregations as once they came into being in the early Church, and as we meet them in the record of the New Testament. As we are placed in the royal priesthood of today more must be said. We now see various non-Christian religious bodies and also a number of Christian denominations. They all have congregations. If we desire to cover them all we may say that a congregation is any group of religious people united to maintain public worship of some kind or other. They are alike only in this one point of keeping up regular public worship. They are divided by the greatest

CONFESSIONAL DIFFERENCES.

Congregations that either reject or pervert the Lord's teaching altogether are plainly antichristian. Congregations that alter more or less of the Lord's teaching are still called Christian in a general way if they retain enough to produce saving faith in Christ. Only those congregations that abide wholly by the Lord's teaching in what they preach and in what they practice are Christian in the full sense of the word. A mark of the latter is that nothing they proclaim or do hinders men from coming to Christ or disturbs their connection with him.

It ought to be very plain that you and I as members of the royal priesthood must be true to Christ and his Word in all things, and that therefore we could remain only in a congregation that teaches men to observe all things the Lord has commanded us, Matth. 28, 20. If there is no congregation of this kind within our reach where we may happen to live, we should do our utmost to found one.

There are two ways of determining the real character of a congregation. Nearly every congregation forms an organization which has a written constitution, recognized even by the authority of the state. In that constitution the congregation declares what it believes and intends to preach and teach. This declaration is its confession. By it we may know what kind of a congregation it is.

Sometimes, however, the written confession is allowed in whole or in part to become a dead letter. Therefore a second test is added to the first. We examine what is actually preached and taught, what is actually practiced and done. By means of these two tests the real character of any congregation can safely be determined.

The Lord himself has combined the public proclamation of his Word, which he committed to us as a royal priesthood, with the gift of

THE CHRISTIAN MINISTRY.

By means of this ministry we as the royal priesthood are to carry out the Lord's bidding concerning all that belongs to the public use of his Word. Each congregation is to call and maintain in its midst a pastor, and to him it shall allot the public work of the Word. The Christian ministry is thus *a divine institution,* an arrangement which the Lord himself has made.

"He gave some, apostles; and some, prophets; and some, evangelists; and some, pastors and teachers." Eph. 4, 11. It is the Lord who made this gift. It is to the Church that he made it, which means the royal priesthood of believers. And the gift consists of the holy office of the ministry as we see it in the work of the apostles and others, all working with the Word in public.

The apostles had an exceptional task in this respect, for which reason also the Lord in person appointed and trained them. They received the gift of divine Inspiration, by which they were to furnish the Church of all ages the Lord's Word and will in written form. Thus we of the royal priesthood are all "built upon the foundation of the apostles and prophets, Jesus Christ himself being the chief corner stone." Eph. 2, 20. We have the New Testament from the apostles. St. Mark and St. Luke, who wrote three of the books of the New Testament, did their work in conjunction with apostles, the former in connection with St. Peter, the latter in connection with St. Paul.

The apostles also had the special duty of getting the Church under way by gathering and organizing the first congregations and arranging their work in detail. We have a full account of how they did this in the historical record of the Acts and in the letters which they wrote to some of the first congregations and several individuals, notably the two pastors Timothy and Titus.

Because of this special work they had the name "apostles," which means ambassadors. Since this work in the nature of the case could be done only once, there has been no succession of apostles in the Church.

The rest of their work continues to the present day. It is the general work of preaching and applying the Word in public. In this work the successors of the apostles are all true Christian pastors.

It was the Lord's own will which the apostles carried out when they induced the first congregations to choose such pastors. St. Paul with the help of Barnabas had the congregations they had gathered in Galatia select "elders," which means pastors, who were then ordained and given charge. Acts 14, 25. St. Paul directed Titus to do the same thing in the island of Crete. Tit. 1, 5. We know how Timothy was the pastor at Ephesus, and how in two letters St. Paul directed him as to the way in which he should do the work of his office. The seven churches in Asia Minor, to whom the Lord addressed brief letters in Rev. 2 etc., all had their pastors, termed "angels" or messengers; and each was responsible for the spiritual condition of his congregation.

Though these pastors were always selected and called by the congregations, their office is constantly termed divine. When St. Paul said farewell to the pastors of Ephesus he told them that it was the Holy Ghost who had made them pastors of that congregation. Acts 20, 28. In speaking of pastors St. Paul counted himself among them and called them "the ministers of Christ and stewards of the mysteries of God." 1 Cor. 4, 1. And in another place he spoke of them "as the ministers of God." 2 Cor. 6, 4.

Thus did Christ establish the Christian ministry. The royal priesthood of belivers received the gift of this holy office, so that by means of it they might properly carry out the Lord's will in the public use of his Word.

The office belongs to us all as a gift from the Lord. Our ownership of it is one of our high prerogatives as priests unto God. We own it conjointly and equally. It is no more yours than it is mine, or mine than it is yours. It belongs to the children in the congregation as much as to their parents, to the women as much as to the men. No one has a right to take it from us.

It is yours and mine for us, together with the others in our congregation to fill, maintain, and support, not for any one of us of himself to assume and exercise. As royal priests we have

THE RIGHT TO CALL

a pastor for our congregation. This means that we jointly elect one who is a royal priest and has the necessary qualifications, and thereby confer upon him the office which the Lord has instituted for his Church and entrusted to our care.

In a way this is like the presidency of our country. The presidential office belongs to the entire nation and every citizen in it. Yet none of us has the right of himself to act as president. By a general election one man is chosen and the office conferred upon him. In this way we all who own the presidency put the office into operation and secure a president for ourselves.

Here, however, we must note certain differences among the members of the royal priesthood.

From the smallest to the greatest all have identical rights. Yet babes and children, though kings and priests unto God as much as their elders, cannot do what is very properly expected of grown people. Nature and bodily

development make a great difference. Sex offers another
difference which in important respects dare not be ignored.
The Lord chose no women apostles, although in the royal
priesthood as then constituted there were most excellent
women, such as Mary Magdalene, Salome the mother of
James and John, and Mary of Bethany. When the apostles
carried out the Lord's will they directed no congregation
to call a woman as a pastor; and when they laid down
the requisites for the pastoral office, 1 Tim. 3; Tit. 1,
these apply only to men, not to women. Speaking of differences, even sickness and health make a difference in
what a royal priest may do in his holy calling.

Besides the natural there are spiritual differences. Parents are to instruct their children, Eph. 6, 4, not the
children their parents. A brother who errs is to be admonished, Gal. 6, 1, not vice versa. Some have the knowledge and gift of teaching, and we gladly use them in
the Sunday School; the others profit by joining the classes.
The women choose from the ablest of their sex such of-
ficers as they need in their societies, and all the women
profit by such a choice. So it is all along.

When it comes to the ministry, only the few men who
are specially trained and qualified are thought of for office
— all others are left out of consideration. Usually too
there is considerable deliberation in making this important
choice.

The differences among the members of the royal priesthood which we have mentioned come out plainly when
meetings are held to transact the regular business of the
congregation and any special business like that of calling
a pastor. Who of all those that have identical spiritual
rights in the congregation shall attend to this particular
task? In other words, who shall have voice and vote
in these congregational meetings?

Evidently the young and immature cannot take part.
Nobody has ever expected it. As far as ability goes the

women might take part. Yet the fact stands, that the apostles who guided the Church under the Lord's own direction never combined men and women in this work. As the husband is the head of his wife and of his family, so the men are the leaders in the management of the congregation. The Lord himself gave them that leadership through his apostles. They are the ones to act for all the rest when a pastor is to be called.

The Lord has never changed Gen. 3, 16, where he laid down for all time the principle, that the husband shall rule the wife. Repeatedly the apostles tell us the same thing: "The husband is the head of the wife." Eph. 5, 23. She is to submit herself, Eph. 5, 22; to reverence her husband, Eph. 5, 33. "The head of the woman is the man." 1 Cor. 11, 3. For this reason silence is enjoined on the women in the Church, 1 Cor. 14, 34, and they are to usurp no authority over the men, 1 Tim. 2, 12-15.

The claim is made that this old arrangement of the Lord does not apply to our modern conditions. Whoever says that sets up the principle that in managing the Church we are no longer to ask, What saith the Lord? but, What do we think suits our modern conditions? In other words, this means that once *the Lord* directed how things should be done, but now *we* direct them ourselves?

Both men and women as priests of God should bow unquestioningly to all of his directions. We violate our priestly position the moment we set aside a single arrangement he has made. And we double the wrong when first we do the unpriestly thing, and then put it upon the Lord as if he had authorized us.

There is all kinds of room in the congregation for the women to use their priestly rights in ways that please the Lord. In fact, there is usually more work than there are saintly hands of women to do that work. What if the men were to crowd themselves into the meetings and activities of the women on the plea of equal rights? Some things are not only wrong, they are at the same time ridiculous.

Priests though we all are, contentions may nevertheless arise. The flesh still clings to us, and the devil will not leave us alone. Now in all truth it is bad enough for men to contend with each other in a congregational meeting. To add the sex factor, men and women, perhaps husbands and wives and daughters clashing with each others, makes the damage far greater.

The Lord was wise indeed when he gave one head to a family — anything with two heads is a monstrosity. He was equally wise when, instead of a double leadership by men and women, he gave the congregation a unit leadership of men, and placed the interests of the women in their care. Happy the congregation where the men faithfully attend to this their priestly trust, encouraged thereto by the women. So shall the Church prosper, and the Lord bestow his favor.

To understand the relation between the royal priesthood and the office of the ministry we must know

WHAT THE CALL ENTRUSTS TO THE PASTOR.

It does not entrust to him any of the rights of the royal priesthood. All of us remain priests as before, all of us have the same rights as before, all of us rest under the same obligations as before. Our prerogatives and duties inhere in our very nature as spiritual priests, hence they cannot possibly be transferred, either to a pastor, or to anyone else.

Whether the pastorate be filled or be vacant does not change the royal priesthood of the congregation one whit. As far as my spiritual priesthood is concerned a pastor takes nothing from it, nor does he add anything to it.

We all as priests own the pastoral office and the powers that belong to it just as much when that office is filled as when for a while it is vacant. We all as citizens own the presidential office of our country and the powers that belong to it just as much when a president holds that office as when he happens to die or is impeached.

We must not identify the royal priesthood and the Christian ministry. They are two, not one. When I help call a pastor I do not by that call transfer to him a part of my own royal priesthood. I keep all my citizenship, and hand over nothing of it, when I vote for some man to be the president of my country.

The call entrusts to the pastor the public preaching of the Word. The Sacraments are part of the Word. So the call includes the public administration of the Sacraments. The power to forgive and to retain sins, called the Power of the Keys, inheres in the Word. So the call includes the public administration of this power. In accord with the Word all the affairs of the congregation and the lives of its members are to be directed. So the call includes this direction — the pastor is to guide us jointly and singly according this Word.

Putting it summarily, the call turns over to the pastor all the public work connected with the Word. It is the Work which rests on the whole congregation, and which it can properly perform only by means of a representative who acts for the whole, namely a pastor.

The pastor who accepts a call remains a royal priest as he was before. His priesthood differs in no way from that of any person in his congregation. By his becoming a pastor it is neither increased nor decreased. What the call does is to give him the pastoral office and the work belonging only to that office. He now has two sets of rights and duties, those of the royal priesthood and those of the Christian ministry. The former are his only as a believer, the latter only as pastor. The former he exercises on his own behalf, the latter only on behalf of the congregation whose call he holds.

No part of the royal priesthood of the members in a congregation is transferred by the call to a pastor. The one thing that is transferred to him is the office which Christ gave to his Church and which each congregation is to put into operation in its own midst.

It is Luther who insisted on the biblical requirement that no man should assume the pastoral office or any part of it without a proper call. "No man taketh this honor unto himself, but he that is called of God, as was Aaron." Heb. 5, 4; Rom. 10, 15. "Let all things be done decently and in order." 1 Cor. 14, 40. It would be the hight of disorder for any one at pleasure to start preaching in public. He would be snatching for himself what he could rightly obtain only by an orderly call. If all were to act in this presumptuous and disorderly fashion there would be Babel in the Church.

While the point of order is important, it does not exhaust what lies in the call. Luther insisted that the chief thing about the call is that the Lord has arranged it. The call is divine because the ministry is a divine institution. When a pastor works under a proper congregational call, the Lord's will is done. That is the chief thing. The congregation is built up spiritually and numerically. That is the second chief thing. In addition there is Christian. order.

When a babe is in imminent danger of death any royal priest in the congregation may baptize it. One of the men should do it; if there is none, one of the women should step in. Likewise where a member is depressed under the sense of sin any brother or sister may offer the consolation of the Gospel, and in the name of Christ bestow the absolution or forgiveness of sin. In neither case is there an interference with the work of the ministry, because the royal priesthood includes the necessary power.

When a pastor arrives he can only endorse what has been done and add his pastoral assurance.

Yet the royal priesthood does not entitle its members to administer Communion to one who is near death's door when no pastor is at hand. The necessity of Baptism for a dying babe is far greater than the necessity of Communion for a dying adult member of the Church. For the babe Baptism is the only means of salvation. Dying unbaptized it would die without any means of salvation. The dying adult has had the Word and the Holy Supper in the past, and his Christian friends may bring him the Word to the very last. There is thus abundant consolation. Then, too, the administration of the second sacrament is more complicated than that of the first. This also has decided the Church to place it only in the hands of competent pastors.

There remains for us to examine

THE RESPONSIBILITY OF PRIESTS AND PASTORS

in relation to the Lord and each other.

As royal priests, standing ever in the presence of our Lord we are wholly and directly responsible to him. We may do nothing either privately or conjointly in a congregational meeting that is not in accord with his will and Word. And we must do whatever he enjoins upon us.

No pastor, and no church body, whatever its size, is able to dispense a single, royal priest from a single Word of the Lord.

Every pastor is doubly responsible to the Lord, first as a royal priest, secondly as a divinely called minister. Heb. 13, 17. Read Rev. 2 and 3 and note how the Lord holds the seven pastors of the seven churches in Asia Minor responsible to himself. A pastor dare preach and teach only in harmony with the Word, and all his other work must equally agree with that Word.

No congregation however large, and no church body however powerful, is able to release a single pastor from a single Word of the Lord.

It is not enough that we as priests and as pastors merely *intend* conscientiously to follow the Word. It is not enough that in our meetings we merely *resolve to obey the Word*. We must *actually do* the Word. "If ye keep my commandments, ye shall abide in my love," — it is the only way. John 15, 10; 14, 15 and 21 and 23. Deut. 18, 19; Acts 3, 23. It is a striking and true saying that the way to hell is paved with good resolutions, those made but not kept.

The Lord pardons ignorance, weekness, error, and many a fault where there is a contrite heart. Will he pardon plain contradictions of his Word, continued disobedience, perversions due to worldly motives such as self-interest, popular demands, and the like? Can he pardon when such deviations are actually made in his holy Name and loudly defended as the true sense of his Word?

The royal priests in a congregation are responsible to their pastor. But only when that pastor brings them the Word. "Remember them which have the rule over you, who have spoken unto you the Word of God," etc. Heb. 13, 7; also 17. If a pastor offers as the Word what is not the Word, we must resist and never yield. Gal. 1, 7-9. If we must mark and avoid those who among the members cause divisions and offenses contrary to the doctrine we have learned from the apostles, Rom. 16, 17, how much more must we resist and avoid a pastor who does this kind of thing? 2 John 10; Jude 3.

The pastor is responsible to his congregation. He has received his call from them. But his responsibility is only secondarily to his congregation, it is primarily to the Lord. He has received his call from the Lord through the congregation. If the congregation or any part of it make demands contrary to the Lord and his Word, the pastor must resist in the name of the Lord. He must remind his people that they as priests and he as pastor are equally responsible to the Lord and dare not swerve from his Word. He dare not yield, though it cost him his office and living.

The ministry is to aid the priesthood in all things spiritual. We need our pastors in countless ways, especially at critical times in our lives. Faithful and zealous pastors are one of the Lord's great gifts to the Church. Woe to those who make the lives and work of such pastors hard. "Obey them that have the rule over you, and submit yourselves: for they watch for your souls, as they that must give account, that they may do it with joy, and not with grief: for that is unprofitable for you." Heb. 13, 17.

The priesthood is to encourage the minister in all his faithful work. Read the greetings St. Paul added in his letter to the Romans, ch. 16, and note how he speaks of those who had helped him and the Church in their labors. "Let him that is taught in the Word communicate unto him that teacheth in all good things." Gal. 6, 6. As royal priests our obligation is to share our earthly wealth with our pastors. St. Paul writes, "If we have sown unto you spiritual things, is it a great thing if we shall reap your carnal things? . . . Even so hath the Lord ordained that they which preach the Gospel should live of the Gospel." 1 Cor. 9, 11 and 14. But love is more than money or a good salary. Love means loyal hearts, support by word and deed in the great work, and the kindly appreciation which turns the pastor's hardest labor into joy.

When the Lord dictated to St John his brief letter to the pastor and congregation in Philadelphia in Asia Minor, Rev. 3, 7-13, he had only commendation for both. Philadelphia thus stands for all time as a model for the right relation of priests and pastor to each other.

Priests and the Book

We might head this chapter "The Layman and his Bible." It will also have to treat of the royal priesthood in connection with the right of private judgment.

Has the layman the right to use the Bible?

May he own it and study it without restriction?

Is he entitled to use it for his devotions, to edify his soul, strengthen his faith, increase his holiness?

Dare he also use the Bible to test what is preached to him by the church, by the clergy, and by his own pastor?

We use the terms "layman" and "clergy" here, because they are customary in this connection. It is quite the same when we ask,

Has the royal priesthood the right to full and unrestricted use of the Bible?

Dare we as kings and priests unto God freely study his Word and by it test without interference all that meets us inside and outside the Church?

Some may think these questions rather useless, because we all not only have our Bibles to-day, but are even admonished to make the fullest use of them. Nor has anybody ever interfered with us in this matter. As for ourselves all that we usually feel in this regard is that we have been remiss in our use of the Sacred Book.

Yet so far from useless are these questions that they are really vital in the highest degree.

In the first place, our right to the Bible has long been authoritatively denied. It cost the severe struggle of the Reformation for us to be free to use our Bibles as we do now. Those who are still under the papacy have this liberty denied them to-day, or have it heavily restricted. We must know these things, so that we may appreciate what it means for us to have the Bible in our own hands, and what a blessing it is for all of us to use it with completest freedom.

In the second place our right has been all along, and is still, interfered with by false authorities.

Some of these authorities are ecclesiastical. They misread the Bible badly on most important points, and then insist that all of us ought to misread it in the same way. They resist all efforts to correct them, splitting up the Christians into different sections, these often contending against each other. Some of these perversions actually empty out all the saving contents of the Bible, so that all who heed such authority lose the very substance of the Christian faith and cease to be members of the royal priesthood altogether.

Again these authorities are secular, headed by men learned in philosophy and science. They demand that their destructive interpretations be put upon what the Bible says. Many of them flatly reject entire parts of the Book, and some cast it aside altogether as entirely without value. And then they insist with the strongest kind of pressure that we must all yield to them and do just as they do.

Certainly, they say, you may read your Bible if you want to! But understand what you read as we tell you to! If you dare to understand it just as it actually reads, you are ignorant, narrowminded, in conflict with reason, medieval, dead-orthodox, unprogressive, unscientific, hopelessly behind modern scholarship!

And they say these things with an air so lofty and superior as if they themselves were almost gods. Superciliously they look down upon us as if we were to be pitied for being so childish as still to take the Bible at its word. Acting so lordly they actually at times make us feel little and cheap, until a look at the Word again reassures us. All their little arrows and popguns will never demolish what the great statesman Gladstone significantly called "the Impregnable Rock of Holy Scripture."

Many who do not really know the Bible are impressed. The damage is great among the callow students in High Schools and Colleges. They allow their precious priestly rights to be badly invaded, and only too often to be snatched away entirely. They let one or more of these false authorities step between them and their God as he would meet them in the Bible. Instead of taking God's own words from his own mouth as he utters them in the Bible, they let one or the other of these ecclesiastical or secular authorities twist his words, or actually deny his words, and perhaps all too late discover the dastardly and deadly wrong that has been done them.

There is thus only too much reason for us to investigate and learn all we can about

OUR SACRED AND PRIESTLY RIGHT TO THE BIBLE.

The result for us should be the most powerful impulse to hold fast our right and to exercise it to the limit of our abilities. It should be an impulse far more effective than all the ordinary admonitions we receive to read and study our Bible.

Let us repeat it — a king has no one above him but God, and a priest has no one between him and God. Every royal priest among us has full and free access to God. He has the right to go to God directly, to deal with God in his own person.

Nobody in the whole world dare say, You must first come to me, and I will tell you what God has to say to you, or whether he has anything to say to you at all! Whoever attempts such a thing snatches your kingship away and makes himself a king over you, turning you into a slave. He robs you of your priesthood and makes himself a priest over you, turning you into a priest-ridden dupe. It is the most ungodly business that has ever been done either inside or outside of the Church.

You have a sample of it in your first mother. Eve had God's own word from his own mouth, not to eat of the forbidden tree. Satan interposed himself between God and her. He questioned the word that God had spoken, Did God really say that? Then he altered the word and denied that Adam and Eve would die if they ate of the tree. Thus our first parents fell. Satan thrust himself between them and God's Word.

Satan has had many agents among men. Among them the Pharisees stand out in the New Testament. Hear Jesus, "Woe unto you, scribes and Pharisees, hypocrites! for ye shut up the kingdom of heaven against men: for ye neither go in yourselves, neither suffer ye them that are entering to go in." Matth. 23, 13. How did they keep men out? By falsifying God's Word. By thrusting themselves and their self-made rules and regulations in between men and God's Word.

At all hazard we must guard our kingship and priesthood. Let no man touch the royal crown and priestly robe given us by God in Baptism. And the one and only way to keep our royal and priestly right intact and uninjured is to exercise it constantly and in the fullest degree.

Here on earth there is one place where we as royal priests meet God face to face. That place is the Bible. When you open the Book you actually open the door to God's presence. When you read any part of that Book you hear God's own voice speaking to you. Every thought, feeling, volition that stirs in your heart as you hear that voice of God is your answer to God. It is both a kingly and priestly act in which you thus engage. And among all the unimportant acts in which men engage there is none so high, so sacred, and therefore so blessed.

It is God himself who grants us this supreme right to meet him face to face in his Word. Every book in the

Bible was written for us to read, study, and apply. The prophets reminded all the people of all the words God had up to that time spoken unto them. "Hear, O Israel!" God himself exclaims. Deut. 6, 4. He even threatens, "Whosoever will not hearken unto my words . . . I will require it of him." Deut. 18, 19.

Can there be anything plainer than Jesus' own command, "Search the Scriptures!" John 5, 39. When the rich man in hell dared to suggest a different authority, Jesus puts this answer into Abraham's mouth, "They have Moses and the prophets; let them hear them!" Luke 16, 29. Why did the Lord through St. Paul praise the Bereans so highly? They "searched the Scriptures daily." Acts 17, 11.

The Psalmist was right, "Thy Word is a lamp unto my feet, and a light unto my path." Ps. 119, 105. And again, "In thy light shall we see light." Ps. 36, 9.

Read the Bible from end to end, never is there any restriction or limitation to this our royal priestly right. There is only the strong admonition, "Let the Word of Christ dwell in you richly in all wisdom!" Col. 3, 16.

There is a mighty reason for granting so great a right to us all. It is because

EVERY PERSON IS RESPONSIBLE TO GOD FOR HIS OWN SOUL.

God created your soul and gave it to you. It is yours, and yet it belongs to God. As your Creator he can never relinquish his right to you and your soul. In the end he is bound to require it of you. Luke 12, 20. Nobody can possibly change this.

Here we have the first reason why God must, and always will, hold you responsible for your soul.

When sin came into the world and tore us away from God he redeemed us. He gave the life and blood of his Only Begotten Son as a price for your soul. He purchased and won it by paying that price. Your soul belongs to God by a double right, that of creation and that of redemption. After paying such a price God is most deeply concerned about your soul. He must ask what you are doing, and in the end what you have done, with your soul. Nobody, let him say or think what he pleases, can ever change this fact.

Here is the second reason why God must, and ever will, hold you responsible for your soul.

Are you leaving your soul benighted, in darkness? Does it still wear the devil's shackles of sin as his slave? Do vices and passions degrade it in mire and filth? Does it find its pleasures away from God in the far country of the sinful world? God holds *you* accountable.

Does your soul walk in the light of God? Are its eyes open to see the blessed paths of righteousness? Has the Son made your soul free? Has it found its place among God's own children in the house of his Church? Is your soul washed clean of all guilt by the blood of your Lord? Is it made beautiful with Christian virtues and adorned with deeds that delight God? If so, you will gladly make answer, and never dream that *you* are not accountable to God.

If God had not given you a soul and had never redeemed your soul, then only might you disclaim this responsibility for your soul and its condition. Now you cannot possibly do so.

All that we have said about our responsibility for our own souls applies to men generally. God judges our souls now, day by day. And there is coming the great final day of judgment for all the world when every human being must appear before Christ and answer to him for his soul.

But all that we have said applies in a special way to us who are kings and priests unto God. We know of his creation and redemption. We meet him face to face in his Word. "Unto whomsoever much is given, of him shall be much required." Luke 12, 48. Our responsibility as a royal priesthood is according to our greater gifts.

Each is responsible for his own soul — a responsibility from which none can ever free himself. And now we must add a second responsibility. We are all responsible also for each other — you for my soul, and I for yours. This is

OUR MUTUAL RESPONSIBILITY.

This too, like the other, we can never shake off.

It is because none of us lives to himself, and none of us dies to himself. We are in constant contact with each other. Whether we intend it, desire it, or not, each of us influences the other. And the supreme point of that contact and influence is in the matter of our souls.

You either help or hurt my soul, and I do the same thing, either or, to yours. Either we lead one another to the Word of God and its salvation, or we bar each other from that Word. Either we lift one another out of the lies of the devil and men, or we help to entangle each other in their meshes.

And for what we do to each other in this respect God holds, and must hold each of us responsible. If I ruin my brother's soul God will require my brother's blood at my hands. "Woe unto the world because of offenses! . . . Woe to that man by whom the offense cometh!" Matth. 18, 7.

Physical murder is a frightful crime, but the murder of a soul is still more frightful. Even neglect to save where we can save is murder. If I can throw a rope to a drowning man and fail to do it, I am guilty of his death. If I see one reaching for a bottle of poison under the impression that it is medicine, and say and do nothing, I am a poisoner. It is exactly the same with a soul that is drowning or taking poison.

This responsibility for the souls of others is added to our responsibility for our own souls. If I were not responsible first of all for my own soul I could not be held responsible for your soul. The same is true of your relation to me. It is thus that the two responsibilities are connected together.

How God measures out this responsibility to each of us he has told us sufficiently in his Word. "That servant which knew his lord's will, and prepared not (himself), neither did according to his will, shall be beaten with many stripes. But he that knew not, and did commit things worthy of stripes, shall be beaten with few stripes." Luke 12, 47-48. "Whoso shall offend one of these little ones which believe in me, it were better that a millstone were hanged about his neck, and that he were drowned in the depth of the sea." Matth. 18, 6.

Some things God has wisely withheld. For there are questions, entanglements, and intricacies connected with our mutual responsibilities which our minds cannot unravel now. Only this is certain, when we at last see the solutions we shall praise God for both his grace and his justice, for the solutions will be absolutely perfect.

What about the heathen who have died without ever hearing his Word? What about children who die without even the possibility of Baptism? What about collective guilt, that of a nation for instance, a church body, a city, a family, and each individual's share in it? God's royal priesthood may well leave these questions to him who alone has the obligation to solve them.

Men have often made

THE EFFORT TO SHIFT THE RESPONSIBILITY

for their own and other men's souls.

That is the old well known papal idea. A spurious ecclesiastical priesthood comes and tells you, We are the responsible people. Place your soul into our keeping. We will insure its safety. Do as we say. We will attend to everything. Do not try to investigate for yourself. Let us decide for you.

How many people do you know who have invested their money on similar assurances, and have miserably lost? Responsibility by proxy is a dangerous thing even in ordinary human affairs. It is fateful in the affairs of the soul.

This papal scheme has its variations, first, wherever human reasoning has secured control in the church, and secondly, wherever human reasoning outside of the churches by means of its philosophy and scientific authority dictates to the soul. *We* know, these men say, you must take our word for it. Our logic settles the matter. Do as we say. You cannot investigate as we have done. Rest easy, and let us decide for you.

Only too many are willing to make such a shift. But can they — really? On the day of judgment will Christ accept them when they tell him that they did not examine his Word themselves, or did not believe it when they did look at it, but listened to other voices instead? And will Christ excuse them for influencing others, by word or example, to follow the same kind of a course, because they thought it better to listen to he reasonings of men than to study the Word?

The simple fact is, there is no real way to shift your responsibiliy. The thing has been tried for ages, and men have imagined that they have done it, great organ-

izations even persuading them to that effect. Always God
holds *you* directly and personally responsible. Not a single
soul escapes. The only thing anyone ever succeeds in is
in fooling himself that he has made the shift. Sooner
or later he finds that that is the empty sum of his success.

For always and always your soul remains your own.
And always and always any influence you exert upon
others is also your own. These two you simply cannot
change. To do so you would have to change your identity.
"Every man shall bear his own burden." Gal. 6, 5.

When the Judge calls your name you will not be able
to send another in your place. If your soul has gone
wrong *you* will suffer. Others may too, for misleading
you. But you will suffer first. If you have misled others,
they will of course suffer. But *you* will certainly not escape.

Adam and Eve lost Paradise. Instead of listening to
God they listened to the serpent. *They* were responsible,
and they had to bear their responsibility. Adam tried
to shift his responsibility to Eve, and Eve to the serpent.
Did they succeed? You know, they did not. To be sure
the serpent too was cursed, but that did not free them
in the least. The deceived always suffer together with
the deceiver, when the final accounting comes.

Trying to shift the responsibility is bad, but *ignoring*
it is, to say the least, equally bad.

There are thousands who pay no attention at all to
their souls. For all the thought they give them they
might as well have no souls at all. They treat their own
flesh and blood, and others too, in the same way. Everything that is spiritual they avoid. If it is pressed upon
them they fend it off. Some do it with mockery in a
cynical way. Pontius Pilate was of this class, with his
fling, "What is truth?" King Agrippa was another, with
his supercilious sneer, "Almost thou persuadest me to be
a Christian," meaning to say, that all St. Paul had said
amounted to nothing. Others, like Felix, are more po-

lite about it, "When I have a convenient season I will call for thee." None of them are interested in the Great Supper, and for every invitation they return an excuse.

There is no sight more appalling than this of souls left to drift through life with never a thought expended upon them — human beings eternally responsible, and acting like brute beasts that know no responsibility. They float down Niagara, throwing the oars away, twining flowers around their heads and singing giddy songs, smiling at the cries that warn them, trailing their figures in the quickening current, until it is — too late!

Go ahead, throw your responsibility on the ash pile! But can you — really? "It is appointed unto men once to die, but after this the judgment." Heb. 9, 27.

Do not try to shift or ignore your responsibility — meet it! But know that there is

ONLY ONE WAY TO MEET YOUR RESPONSIBILITY.

It is by means of the Bible. Or, stating it more completely, by making use of your priestly right to see for yourself what God has to say to you regarding your own soul and the souls of others.

As long as you fail to use this right, or let someone prevent you from using it, you are not meeting your priestly responsibility to God, and when called to account will stand self-condemned.

The blessed thing is that the God who judges you today, and will judge you at the last day, has fully told in the Bible how you may be safe in that judgment. He has done more. In the Bible he himself comes to you to make you safe, and to let you enjoy now already all the comfort, assurance, and joy that safety gives.

This, then, is God's way for you to meet your responsibility. There is no other way. Meeting it so, it will indeed be met. As a king with nobody above you but God and as a priest with nobody between you and God, he wants to meet you in his Word, speak to you, reach out the hand of his love and grace to you, and by that love and grace make you safe forever.

It is another way of saying that he wants you to exercise your priestly

RIGHT OF PRIVATE JUDGMENT,

go personally to him in his Word, hear and judge yourself what he has to tell and to give you.

We call it "private" judgment in distinction from the official judgments of the clergy or some organized church body. "Private" too, as for your own soul, where the clergy and the church body act officially for others.

We must know that Luther and the Reformation secured three immense blessings for us, those originally given to the Church by Christ himself. We call them *the principles of the Reformation* — principles, because all three of them govern our entire spiritual life and everything connected with it.

The first is, God's Word alone is to say what we are to believe and do.

The second is, by grace alone through faith in Christ are we justified (pardoned) and saved.

The third is, you for yourself alone are to judge what God's Word declares and offers you for your salvation.

We often state these three principles more briefly:

1) The Scriptures alone.

2) By grace alone.

3) You in your own person alone.

While we distinguish three principles, the three belong together and form one grand unit. It is the third that ties a cord around the other two.

If God's Word alone is to say what I am to believe and do, then I myself and for myself must have the right to go to that Word and judge what it says. Again, if I am justified and saved by grace alone, through faith in Christ, then I myself and for myself must have the right to go to God's Word and there find that grace, pardon, and salvation.

Without the right thus to judge for myself the other principles of the Reformation would be ineffective for me.

Men may tell me, This is what God's Word says! How can I be sure if I dare not go and judge for myself? Men may tell me, This is how you are justified and saved! How can I be sure if I dare not go and judge for myself?

With my own soul at stake, I must demand this right for myself.

Thank God, then, for the right of private judgment!

But now let us be sure that we do not twist this precious right and make it mean

WHAT IT DOES NOT AND DARE NOT MEAN.

The enemies of this right constantly pervert it in order the more easily to deprive us of it. And many who intend to maintain and exercise this right nevertheless misunderstand it.

The right of private judgment is nevermore the right to interpret the Bible as you, or as I, may please. God never gave us a right like this, that you may say of a Scripture statement, This is what it means! while I may say, No; this is what it means! You dare not insist, I am entitled to my view! while I insist, I am just as much entitled to mine!

Such a perversion of the right of private judgment makes a putty nose out of Scripture, one that each man can give a twist to suit himself. Any supposed right like this is a farce. It is worse, an insult to God and his Word.

This is how all sorts of false interpretations have arisen, splitting the church into warring camps. Each sect insists that it has a right to its interpretation, and all of them insist that their contradictory interpretations are the true meaning of God's Word.

It does not take much wisdom to see that all this is wrong, likewise sadly deplorable. To abolish this abuse the radical remedy is offered, that there must be a central authority among men which alone shall have the right to say what the Bible or any of its statements really mean. It is the papal solution. The pope claims to be that central authority, and an authority set up in the Church by God himself. But the moment we stoop to such an authority the whole right of private judgment is gone, our royal priesthood itself is gone. And on top of it all the authority of the Bible itself is gone. The remedy thus is worse than the disease it claims to cure. No longer does God himself by means of his Word rule in the Church, but this human authority rules with its decisions on what the Bible does, and does not, say we are to believe and do.

No; neither you nor I dare interpret the Bible as we please, nor dare any man make us interpret it as he pleases.

But if none of us dares to interpret the Bible as he pleases,

WHAT DOES THE RIGHT OF PRIVATE JUDGMENT MEAN?

It means that you and I and all men dare interpret the Bible only in one way, namely the one way laid down by the Bible and in the Bible itself.

Every sentence in the Bible has only one meaning, not two or more, not possibly this or possibly that meaning. And when we go to the Bible every last one of us dare find only that one true and actual meaning, and not a single thing besides.

The Bible is one. Its divine Author is one. All its teachings are one. The Bible never says one thing in one place and a contrary thing in another place. It is no house divided against itself. It is no Chinese puzzle. And the right of private judgment is this, that we dare find only this one harmonious truth in the Bible, and never a thing that clashes with any part of this truth.

If ever we are in doubt as to what a statement in the Bible means, we must go to the Bible itself for the answer. If what the Bible says in one place seems to us to contradict what it says in another place, we must go to the Bible itself to have the difficulty removed. If in either case we are unsuccessful we must know that the real answer and solution is there nevertheless in the Bible, and that it is our ignorance which fails to find what we need.

Let us learn once for all that *the Bible is its own interpreter.*

Not you with your reasoning wise or otherwise. Not philosophers and scientists with their logic, laws, theories, hypotheses, and deductions. Not popes with their decrees and *ex cathedra* pronouncements. Not ancient councils, or modern synods, conferences, diets, assemblies. They all may err. Any number of them have erred.

Even when a man, say the faithful pastor of your own congregation, tells you truly what the Bible says, your right demands for you that you see for yourself that he is telling you truly. The people of Berea are praised because, when St. Paul brought them the Gospel, they on their part "searched the Scriptures daily, whether those things were so." Acts 17, 11.

The purest creed has our faith only because we ourselves see that that creed is true to the Bible.

As the Bible interprets itself, so our right of private judgment is to accept that interpretation alone, and no other, whatsoever it may be, or whencesoever it may come.

Moreover, *the Bible is perfectly able to interpret itself*.

It is so clear in its statements that it takes special ingenuity and real ignorance to spoil its meaning.

In hundreds of cases it is not a question at all, what the Bible itself actually says and means — that is as clear as can be; the question is, Are you ready to believe what the Bible says so clearly, or is there something in you that objects? Men twist or deny what the Bible says, not because its meaning is hard to get at, but because they dislike that meaning, and are determined to have one that suits them.

In all points of real inportance for your soul the Bible repeats its meaning in a number of different places, and each repetition is an interpretation.

Here it states a thing briefly, but there it explains at length. Now it uses a positive form, again it adds a negative for greater clearness. What it states figuratively in one place it states literally in the next. In fact, it uses all the forms of which human speech is capable, so that its meaning shall be clear. That foxy diplomat Talleyrand once said that language is intended to hide one's meaning. Lying diplomats may use it in that way. God's purpose is to reveal. He made language. Shall he not be able to use it perfectly for his purpose?

Do you want to know what sin is? The Bible tells you in a hundred places, and all of them agree. Do you want to know what pardon is? The Bible is full of statements that tell you, and they all agree. So you can get scores of answers to all proper questions. Who is Christ? What is regeneration, conversion, sanctification, resurrection, salvation? Who made the world, and how?

Is there a heaven and a hell, and what are they like? Are there angels and devils, and how did the latter come to be?

The Bible is full of illustrations. And the object of all of them is just one, namely to make something clear. There are ever so many historical examples, every one inserted to make us understand fully.

The Sacred Book is a vast emporium, all its counters, cases, and shelves full of treasures, all arranged that we may freely go in and buy without money or price.

The Bible especially delights to answer the supreme question of the soul, How may I escape from sin and obtain everlasting life?

In the face of all this it is a monstrous slander to call the Bible a dark book. It is the one source of light and life for the whole world, and beside it there is no other. There are so many treasures of truth in it that the brightest mind in the longest life will not be able to garner them all.

Yet there are certain things which the Bible does not tell us. It is for you and me humbly to stop at this boundary line. Some things our limited minds cannot possibly graps now, and some things are not good for us to know now. What is the origin of sin and evil? No human mind can fathom the mystery. When will judgment day come? God does not want you to know. All the tangled mysteries of divine providence are beyond us.

God is our Father, and we are his little children. As earthly fathers tell their little ones only about what is good for them, so our heavenly Father does with us. Bless his wisdom and love, and be happy as his children!

All of us have the identical priestly right to go to the Bible and there to see and judge for ourselves. Yet we cannot all exercise this right in the same way. This is due to the natural and spiritual differences among us. Consider, then,

YOUR PART IN USING THE RIGHT OF PRIVATE JUDGMENT.

There is a decided difference in age and development. Children are immature. They begin with the alphabet. They receive the milk of the Word. What St. Peter wrote of beginners in the faith applies to children in a natural way. "As newborn babes desire the sincere milk of the Word, that ye may grow thereby," 1 Pet. 2, 2. Meat is for strong men.

All beginners in the faith are in the same class. "First the blade, then the ear, after that the full corn in the ear." Mark 4, 28. It is the natural law of spiritual development in the royal priesthood.

What a mistake to ignore it! Can one climb the top steps before he has ascended the lower ones? Can one master algebra and geometry before he knows arithmetic? Yet what is so self-evident in natural learning is often ignored in spiritual learning. Some have tried to solve the hardest things in the Bible first, and then, when they failed, threw the Bible aside as a useless book.

Education makes a difference. While one who has learned little more than to read may get from the Bible all that he needs, many things in the Sacred Volume are necessarily beyond him. He fills the cup that he has; if it were larger he could fill it just as easily.

This is why the Lord gives us teachers of his Word, and why teaching is and ever will be such a glorious work in the royal priesthood. Fathers and mothers are to train

up their children in the nurture and admonition of the
Lord. Eph. 6, 4. Experienced Christians and especially
pastors are to help others in building up their faith on
the Bible. Even pastors have conferences and synods
where they meet to further each other in the Word. Read
the story of the first conference in Jerusalem, Acts 15.
Ever those who know more are to impart to those who
know less.

Yet every bit of this teaching is to lead into the Word
and into the Word alone. The little feet of child faith
are to stand on the Rock of Ages just as much as the
strong feet of the greatest Bible theologian.

No greater mistake can be made than to found the
faith even of a mere child on its parent's word, or the
faith of a congregation on its pastor's word. Human
teachers may indeed lead the way, but only as the Sama-
ritan woman led the way for the people in her village.
They testified, "Now we believe, not because of thy saying: for we have heard him ourselves, and know that this
is indeed the Christ, the Savior of the world." John 4, 42.

Your part, then, in using the priestly right of private
judgment is indicated by the measure of saving knowledge
you have acquired from the Bible. If you have only little
as yet, use that little faithfully for your own soul and
for others. If you have much, use it all with the same
faithfulness for yourself and others.

As between pastors and laymen there is only the difference of the call and the office. Both laymen and pastors go to the Bible by right of the royal priesthood,
using their right of private judgment in an identical way.
But the pastors also go to the Bible by reason of their
divine call to the holy office in order "to feed the Church of
God, which he hath purchased with his own blood." Acts
20, 28.

The more our right of private judgment is recognized and used as God means us to use it, the more will the Church grow in the Word, in grace, in knowledge and wisdom, in the confession of the truth and genuine spirituality, in inner unity and oneness, and in power to win greater triumphs in the world.

Priest and School

What has the royal priesthood to do with schools and education?

Nothing at all! Someone may answer.

Yet the true answer is, Just about everything!

To be sure, the secular view of education is the one that generally prevails in our country to-day. And the secular reasons for educating everybody are the ones that now bulk in men's minds. It should not surprise us even to meet the idea, that earthly and secular considerations have produced the idea of universal education.

Historically this is a mistake. Modern education begins with the Reformation. In particular, the grand impulse to give everybody as good an education as possible, and to provide all the necessary facilities for doing this dates from the spiritual renewal that began in the period of the Reformation.

We might show this in detail and at length by leafing through the pages of history. Since our discussion is limited to a survey of principles, what they really are and what they involve, we omit the history connected with them. For us just now the fact is enough.

THE SUPREME REASON FOR EDUCATION IS SPIRITUAL.

The soul interests were the ones that first called for universal education. Only when afterwards the State, completely separated from the Church, assumed the general educational obligation, were the soul interests crowded out by secular interests. But in spite of this actual crowding out, as we see it to-day in our state system of lower and higher schools, the fact will ever stand, that it is really the Gospel, with the three great principles of the Reformation as defining the controlling ideas of the Gospel, which demands a proper degree of education for every human being born into this world.

In other words, it is the royal priesthood of believers in the Gospel which rightfully voices, and of necessity must voice the demand for the education of the race.

Because I am answerable to God for my soul, I must be able to read, study, and make God's Word my own.

Because God has given his Word to me, and has added the right for me myself to go to that Word, I must have education enough to do so. My priestly right to private judgment demands education.

And this right which as a priest of God I am bound to demand for myself compels me to require education for all of my fellow men.

All of them, like myself, are answerable to God for their souls. If they do not realize it, the fact still remains, and will always assert itself.

God gave his Word and Gospel to the whole world. It is the supreme concern of every human being. If many do not realize it, this again does not change the fact a particle, and again the fact will always assert itself.

God wants every man to go directly to his Word and there learn for himself what God has to say and to give to him. Whether men do it or not, the intention of God is none the less a fact. And again this fact will assert itself.

Here is the true reason for universal education. We may put it into three brief expressions:

1) Responsibility for your soul.
2) God's Word for the world.
3) The right of all men to that Word.

These three spiritual reasons apply to all men equally. They may or may not be recognized. Their conclusive force is not altered thereby. In the royal priesthood they are and will be recognized. It is our high prerogative to recognize the supreme reason for universal education, to proclaim it abroad, and to make it effective in life as completely as we can.

In all the world there are no secular reasons for education that can equal or supersede the true spiritual reason. The spiritual reason stands supreme.

Its supremacy has often been challenged. The good thing is that no challenge that ever was made, or ever can be made, is able to alter the underlying facts.

Now it need not surprise us in the least that secular considerations are both put ahead of the spiritual one, and made to usurp its place entirely. So many people forget that they even have a soul. How can its needs and interests count with them? This life is the sum of their thoughts, and failing to provide for the life to come they lose the best even in this life, and deem themselves wise in thus cheating themselves.

Long ago Jesus said, "Whosoever will save his life shall lose it; but whosoever shall lose his life for my sake and the Gospels, the same shall save it." Mark 8, 35. And again, "He that loveth his life shall lose it; and he that hateth his life in this world shall keep it unto life eternal." John 12, 25. His words are incontrovertibly true. Devote every energy only to this temporal life; it is the surest way to lose both eternal life and the real things of the temporal life.

Men may educate for the lower reasons which center in the temporal life, and not in the soul. They may hush the cry of the soul, and bury it under an avalanche of materialistic argument. The soul and its interest nevertheless remain supreme.

The sad thing is that many Christians are afflicted with this blindness. They want their children to be educated in order to get on well in the world — and that is about all. Christ has answered them long ago, "What shall it profit a man, if he shall gain the whole world, and lose his own soul?" Mark 9, 36.

Nobody can ever change these facts — they will stand till doomsday:

The soul is more than the body.

The spiritual life is more than the physical and temporal.

Spiritual treasures are more than earthly.

The Word of God is above all human wisdom.

Salvation is priceless.

And now consider the royal priesthood in this matter. We at least are all to know these unalterable facts. We at least are ever to proclaim them anew to a deluded world. We at least are to be governed by them. If we who have the light let it go out in our own hearts and lives, it will be dark indeed in the world.

But it is only one side of the truth to recognize the supremacy of the spiritual interests of men. It is only part of the truth to say that the spiritual interests demand education for all. Our royal priesthood leads us farther. It adds the other side, the second part. Rightly understood,

THE SPIRITUAL INTERESTS FOR EDUCATION INVOLVE ALL OTHER INTERESTS.

We are used to contrasting the soul and the body. We put over against each other the earthly and the spiritual. We weigh, as Jesus himself does, the gain of the whole world against the loss of the soul.

This is necessary for many purposes, for men always choose the wrong side of the scales.

We must follow Jesus when he also does the other thing, namely combine soul and body, earthly and spiritual values, the gain of the soul with the gain of the good things of this life. He does it when he bids us, "Seek ye first the kingdom of God, and his righteousness; and all these things shall be added unto you." Matth. 6, 33.

It is a mistake then to think only of the soul, and ignore and neglect the body. God himself combined them. Did not Christ save the body as well as the soul?

It is a mistake to prize only the spiritual treasures, and to despise the earthly treasures. Are not the earthly also the gifts of God? Did not Jesus teach us to pray for our daily bread? Remember how Luther defines what all lies included in "bread," "Such as food, drink, clothing, shoes, house, home, fields, cattle, money, goods, a pious spouse, pious children, pious servants, pious and faithful rulers, good government, good weather, peace, health, discipline, honor, good friends, faithful neighbors, and the like." What is mere bread, even bakeries full of it, if we lack everything else for a happy and safe existence?

Keeping these things in mind we will see that to educate for the soul's sake is at the same time to educate for the body's sake.

To educate for the Word is to educate for all that the Word covers, our entire earthly life.

To educate in order that we may exercise competently our priestly right of private judgment, is to educate in order that we may guide efficiently our entire lives as priests of God according to that judgment.

The sacred, priestly hands that hold the Bible are the hands that will use all things as the Bible bids. The sacred, priestly hearts that receive the truth of the Bible are the hearts that will apply that truth in every part of life.

Is it manual labor, merchandizing, manufacture, business of some kind? Is it money, property, or goods? Is it teaching, medicine, law, science, theology, or some form of learning? Is it a child's round of life, a wife in the home, a man amid stress and labor? Is it personal, family, municipal, national, or Church affairs? Is it a question of mine and thine? Is it one of power and sway over others? Is it the light of happiness, or the clouds of sickness, loss, sadness and sorrow? No matter what it is, always and always the education that fills the soul with the light and power of the Word of God, will by that very act also purify the motives and direct aright the volitions that enter into everything else in life.

To-day scientists like to talk about laws, in fact they swear by laws. Well, there is a "law" back of what we have said thus far, we might even call it a mathematical "law," because it is so inexorable. It is that the whole contains the part, the greater includes the less. The interests of the soul include all the interests of life. The education that takes full care of the soul interests by that very fact takes care of all the interests of life.

The reverse is equally true. The less cannot possibly include the greater, no part has ever equalled its whole. To educate only for temporal interests is to leave out the chief interests of man. In fact, to educate only for temporal interests is not even to take proper care of these.

We are ready now to look at

THE SECULAR REASONS FOR EDUCATION,

as they are advanced to-day and as we of the royal priesthood commonly meet them.

The first of these secular reasons is *the advantage of education for the earthly life.*

Stated baldly, secular education means money and the countless things money can buy. Taking a higher level, secular education means enrichment of life socially, intellectually, esthetically. Climbing to the very pinnacle, secular education may mean power, honor, and fame.

Ignorance negatives all these advantages. Widespread ignorance is the mother of squalor, disease and superstition. It is the helpless prey of evil forces. Ignorance reacts on itself, and the reaction is steadily downward.

So men have come quite generally to prize and seek education irrespective of their souls and any soul interest.

The second secular reason is *the need of intelligent citizens for the state*. The state cannot prosper without sufficiently educated citizens.

This is especially true of a republic like ours. Only educated citizens are able to govern themselves without making a wreck of things. Even so their efforts leave much to be desired.

This is certainly no new wisdom. Years ago Luther said, "Even if there were no soul, and men did not need schools and the languages for the sake of Christianity and the Scriptures, still, for the establishment of the best schools everywhere, both for girls and boys, this consideration is sufficient, namely that society, for the maintenance of the civil order and the proper regulation of the household, needs accomplished and well-trained men and women."

The secular reasons for education are weighed best in connection with the actual education they have produced. We ourselves are face to face with an

EDUCATION COMPLETELY SECULARIZED

and divorced not only from the Bible but from all religion.

In a way this secularization had to occur when the State took over the work of education. For one of the principles of our government is the complete separation of Church and State. With a State that must leave religion entirely alone, the State schools necessarily omit religion.

Beside the constitutional principle involved there is the practical situation of a multiplicity of religious beliefs and organizations among our citizens, to which we must add the lack of all positive religion on the part of a considerable number. If the great body of our citizens were of one religious conviction, this might be different. As the situation actually is, even if the State were in a position to attempt religious teaching, there is absolutely no way to determine what that religious teaching should be.

Thus State education, by a double necessity, is entirely secular. Any religious teaching and training that is done must be apart from the State schools. It is relegated entirely to the family circle or to such provisions as the Church may be able to provide under the circumstances.

We are ready now to examine

THE RESULTS OF SECULAR EDUCATION.

By its very nature this education gravitates to an alarmingly low level. With God, the Word of God, all the interests of the soul, and even religious sanctions of any kind omitted from the educational field, what is there left? Nothing but the transient temporalities of this life. Everything now is only of the earth, earthy. The very power to rise above this low level is gone.

One of the outstanding results of secular education is the loss of moral power. The real sanctions of morality, even in a broad sense, are religious. Genuine godly motives, Christian virtues and spiritual actions flow only from the Bible. An education devoid of religion is an education devoid of moral power. Unless those who receive this sort of an education supply the moral lack by some other means, they are left morally impotent.

Education, moreover, is cumulative in effect. The schooling of one generation after another without religious and moral training tends to deplete and gradually to dissipate the moral forces originally available among the people. As far as secular education is concerned, there are no powers in it even to check this steady moral drain and decline, to say nothing of building up the moral forces in men's lives.

No stream ever rises above it source. This law holds good in education and educational results. People whose education has never lifted them above the transient temporalities of life can at best remain only on this low level with all that they may attain in their lives.

A man may pile up millions by means of his secular education, but he will be able to devote his money only to the transient things in life. Secular education may make me an Edison, but by the power of that education I will never myself rise, or raise anyone else, above electricity. I may become a great scientist, but when all the wonders of earth, air, and the heavens speak to me of the glory of God, their language to me will be a foreign tongue. I may become a king, a president, a great statesman, and have my name immortalized on the pages of all future school histories, as a benefactor of my nation, but in the history of the Kingdom of God my name will appear beside no victories and no blessings, in fact it will not appear at all.

The highest results of secular education in the most favored human lives cannot rise an inch above the mere temporal things of human existence. Even the desire to rise higher will be squelched as far as the results of such education are concerned.

Secular education in losing the moral sanctions of religion, and in particular of the Word of God, loses not only the moral impulses which lift men's lives and attainments up to God, it also loses the moral restraints which keep men from using their acquirements for base and evil ends. An education that increases a man's ability without giving him genuine moral force is in its very nature dangerous. The educated rascal is worse than his ignorant brother.

If the man who eventually commands millions is left by his very education to become evil, he may rob thousands, corrupt and debase other thousands, debase the high as well as the low, spoil even the government of a nation by his power and bribes. The materialistic scientist by his greater ability robs lesser men of their faith in God and religion. A conscienceless ruler and statesman may derail and wreck his own nation.

A sword in the wrong hand is a deadly thing. How much of the crime that runs rampant through our land is a result of an education that by its very nature is powerless in religion and morals?

There is another group of results that dare not be ignored.

While secular education is theoretically neutral as far as religion is concerned, it is practically unable to remain neutral.

To ignore religion is to hurt it in the end. To set the Bible and its teachings aside for one generation of children after another, is to set it aside practically for the duration of their lives. This is exactly the result of secular education for great masses of our people. Even the most zealous mission work of all kinds has been unable to nullify this educational result. Indifference to the Bible and, in fact, to all religious appeal is widespread. Many may think, it is due to the atmosphere. It is — to the atmosphere of a non-religious education. Incline the twig, and the tree is bent. As the trickling fountain, so the rolling stream.

With a secularized education we are become a nation that has the Bible, and yet has it not.

Our secularized education has not been content with its silent and indirect support of irreligion. It has advanced to the open attack on religion in many quarters, in particular to the attack upon the bulwark of all true religion, the Bible.

Sporadic and incidental attacks of this kind there have been many all along in the progress of secular schooling. Irreligious teachers — and there have always been many — simply could not refrain from wicked flings at biblical teachings.

Years ago a little lad came to the writer after Sunday School with the question, Is there a hell? Why did he ask such a question? My teacher in school said that nobody now believes any more that there is a hell! This is a typical case. Irreligious teachers never have had any compunction about destroying religious faith in children. They have often been very successful.

At present the irreligious forces in our secular schools high and low have discovered and mobilized an engine destructive of all religion beyond any weapon they have ever wielded before. Until the pseudo-scientific notion of evolution began to spread in educating circles the attacks on religion were underhand and more incidental. Now they are open and bold, concerted and convinced of complete success. All that is hostile to religion, and espcially to the Bible, rallys around the propaganda of evolution.

They would feed it to the babies with their milk. The little tots are not to believe that God made them in his own image, but that they are the distant descendents of brute beasts. Imagination is brought in and pictures the process in vivid detail as if there were no shadow of doubt. All humanity must be blessed with this delusion, or else, it seems, the race will perish in ignorance.

What the end will be, who can tell?

Thus far have we come with our completely secularized
Thus far have we have come with our completely secularized schools! Secularization has advanced to open irreligion

SECULAR EDUCATION JUDGED

Every effort to make good the moral delinquency of
secular education pronounces judgment upon it. And there
have been any number of such efforts.

The State supports secular education. But it is a detri-
ment, to say no worse, to the State itself to send its young
citizens out into life without proper moral anchorage.
The man who knows only legal, and no moral, restraints
is a danger even to the State. A growing citizenship of
this type may well alarm those who have the true welfare
of the State and the furtherance of the higher interests of
society at heart.

The effort has thus been made to introduce some form
of moral teaching into the State schools. Whether people
realized it or not, that effort in every case was an indictment of secular education.

Thus far the effort has proved abortive. No adequate
system of morals has been found that could be effectively
taught in secular schools.

Again, the effort has been made to enlist the cooperation
of the churches. And again, whether people realized it
or not, this new effort repeated the indictment against
secular education as such.

The scheme is to release the pupils from secular teaching
at a specific time in order that those who desire may
receive religious and moral teaching at the hands of qualified teachers provided by the churches. Up to the present
no great headway has been made in introducing this
scheme.

There are natural difficulties. The great diversity of
religious conviction combined with the total indifference

toward religion on the part of many, complicate the working out of the scheme. Then also, too many of the churches by long training are indifferent even as regards their own children and have no trained teaching force at hand to do the work proposed. Finally, there is the indifference, and sometimes hostility, of the secular school authorities toward any division of teaching like the one indicated by this scheme. The combination of these difficulties has quite generally blocked the introduction of religious teaching by the agency of the churches.

The worst indictments against the secular school system have been made in the legal field.

In at least two states of our country the effort was put forth to crush all private schools teaching religion and to force all children up to a certain age to attend only the secular schools of the State. Any laws to this effect are plainly unconstitutional. The effort to pass such laws and to violate the very constitution of our country, reveals, as hardly anything else can, the hostility against all religion that has grown up under the secular education our State schools have fostered.

In one of our states the battle against evolution in the schools was waged in the courts. The legal battle was won for that state. It commanded the attention of the entire nation. By the verdict of the daily press in the nation that battle was lost. Shut out legally in the State of Tennessee evolution reigns without legal restraint, supported by the press, in the schools of the other states. The fact is both an indictment and a judgment.*

We began by saying that every effort to make good the moral deficiency of secular education amounts to a verdict against that education. We must now add that this education, by surrendering so completely to evolution

* Since this was written other moves have been made in other states, either to pass laws against teaching evolution, or, to prevent their passage. The development is still in progress.

seals that verdict. Evolution is the death of all true morality and moral teaching. For the brute descent of man always must include a morality corresponding to that brute descent, thus on principle shutting out the true morality which comes not from beneath, not from the brute, but from above, from God and the revelation of his Holy Word.

We may now make

THE FINAL DECISIVE COMPARISON.

1) There is the *soul,* the center and pinnacle of human existence, and there are the distinctive interests of the soul.

The royal priesthood demands an education that fully meets the needs of the soul. Secular education knows and cares nothing for the soul.

To the rich fool God said, "Thou fool, this night *thy soul* shall be required of thee: then whose shall those things be which thou hast provided?" Luke 12, 20.

2) There is *the round of human life* with the soul at its center.

The royal priesthood calls for an education that fills this round of life, from its center to its farthest circumference. Secular education knows and cares only for the outer and transient things in this round of human life.

"Godliness is profitable unto all things, having promise of the life that now is, and of that which is to come." 1 Tim. 4, 8.

3) There is *God and his Word.*

The royal priesthood uses both as vitally necessary for education. Secular education omits both, on principle, as vital forces in its teaching.

"The fear of *the Lord* is the beginning of knowledge."

Prov. 1, 7. "The fear of *the Lord* is the beginning of wisdom." Prov. 9, 10. *"All Scripture* is given by inspiration of God, and is profitable for doctrine, for reproof, for correction, for instruction in righteousness: that the man of God may be perfect, thoroughly furnished unto all good works." 1 Tim. 3, 16-17.

4) There is *the moral side of human life,* which really penetrates every part of that life.

The royal priesthood demands of education that it furnish true moral power, right moral standards, effective moral stimuli, safe moral restraints. Secular education has heard of these things, but has always sought them on the lower levels where they cannot possibly be found.

"Wherewithal shall a young man cleanse his way? By taking heed thereto according to thy Word." Ps. 119, 9. "Bring them up in the nurture and admonition of the Lord." Eph. 6, 4.

5) There is *the interest of the State and good government.*

The royal priesthood wants education to instil loyalty for God's sake, backed by divine sanctions. Secular education aims only at a loyalty of natural patriotism and has to be content with that.

"Let every soul be subject unto the higher powers. For there is no power but of God: the powers that be are ordained of God." Rom. 13, 1.

6) There is the question of *universal education,* the right of every human being to at least a fair share of education.

The royal priesthood bases this right on all that it must claim for the soul, the round of life, the Bible, true morality, and loyal citizenship. It is the royal priesthood that possesses the real reason for universal education. Secular education is able to base this right only on the temporal needs of the individual and on the temporal needs of society and the State.

"Wisdom is the principal thing; therefore get wisdom: and with all thy getting get understanding." Prov. 4, 7.

In conclusion, the royal priesthood cannot put its demands for universal education on a lower level. Where it is properly enlightened and efficiently led it will use the means in its power to provide the education that measures up to its demands.

Priest and Citizen

I am both a king and a priest before my Lord God, but in the eyes of my government I am merely a citizen.

In my spiritual life I have no one above me but God and no one between me and God. In my civil life I have the whole civil authority of my government, together with the officials who administer that government, above me.

As a royal priest only one law binds me, namely God's Word. But as a citizen all the laws of my government bind me.

Yet there is no duality. I and my life are not split in two. There is no clash between my priesthood and my citizenship. For my Lord God himself by his Word bids me obey my government; and my government on its part leaves me free to obey God and his Word.

Look at it in another way.

God and his Word govern my entire being and life, my spiritual life as a royal priest, my earthly citizenship, and every other part of my life, everything in my family relation, my business activity, my friendships and associations, my sorrows and my pleasures. There is nothing in which I am not subject to God and his Word. This divine control is complete, absolute, one grand unit.

My government, on the other hand, controls only a small part of my life, namely my earthly citizenship, the outward relation I bear to my fellow citizens. My government has nothing to say about my religion, except that it shall not conflict with my citizenship. It has nothing to say about my family life, my business affairs, my friendships, my sorrows and pleasures, except again in so far as they must not clash with the civil law. There is a great deal in my life in regard to which my government has nothing whatever to say to me, and does not pretend to have. Its control is decidedly limited.

This is as it should be.

The connection between my spiritual priesthood and my earthly citizenship becomes clearer when we note that

EARTHLY GOVERNMENT IS ORDAINED BY GOD.

St. Paul writes with all positiveness to the Christians at Rome under the imperial government of that time, "Let every soul be subject unto the higher powers. For there is no power but of God. The powers that be are ordained of God." Rom. 13, 1.

It is God who so made man, and so shaped the relations of men to each other, that government is both necessary and inevitable. He thus wills it, approves it, or, as St. Paul puts it, he "ordained" it.

Government, or the State in the sense of government, is rightly said to be a divine institution.

St. Paul directs the preacher Titus on this point, "Put them in mind to be subject to principalities and powers, to obey magistrates, to be ready to every good work." Tit. 3, 1.

St. Peter does exactly what St. Paul bids Titus do, when he writes to the Christians in all Asia Minor, "Submit yourselves to every ordinance of man for the Lord's sake: whether it be to the king as supreme; or unto governors, as unto them that are sent by him for the punishment of evildoers, and for the praise of them that do well. For so is the will of God," etc. 1 Pet. 2, 13-15.

God's Word thus puts government on a high plane. It has divine sanction.

Whether kings, governors, magistrates, or the citizens, know it or not, this divine sanction is none the less a fact. They all ought to know it, for their own good. We as royal priests do know it and act according to this knowledge. For us the good that lies in the great fact is realized.

Those who do not know God's Word, or who foolishly disregard it invent their own theories regarding government. Every one of these theories is inferior to the actual fact that government is by divine sanction.

When men guess in their blind wisdom they always guess too low. God made man in his own image; man's wisdom thinks, he is derived from the brute — low indeed. God sent his Son into the world, man's wisdom makes the guess that Jesus was only an ordinary human being — again low indeed. God bestows salvation as a free gift from heaven; man's wisdom, when it thinks of salvation at all, banks on the guess that he must build up his own salvation in the dust of earth — about as low a theory as could be conceived. So with government.

Whoever lets go of the exalted divine facts revealed as such in the Word, puddles around with his theories in the mud.

They tell us, government is an outgrowth of the brute herd idea with its herd leaders. Again we are told, government is an evolution of human intelligence. Still others imagine that government is due to the consent of the governed. Always they look down, never up. Always they seek the explanation beneath, never above. It is enough to make one weep.

God made man so that man cannot dispense with government. It exists by divine sanction.

No nation could possibly consent to abolish all government and henceforth do without it. Anarchy is a hallucination, to say no worse. Some form of government may be cast off, but at once a new form takes its place. If there should be an interval it is one of terror. Nations and communities may break up, but each piece will almost automatically settle on some type of government.

Yet no special form or kind of government has been decreed by God. The Bible speaks of patriarchal government, small kingdoms, and great empires composed of lesser states. Yet no one form has exclusive divine sanction. The Bible does not speak of republics, democracies, parliaments, or congresses, simply because none of these existed in Bible lands and times. These other forms are in no way rejected by the Bible.

The expressions used in the Scriptures are broad enough to include all forms of government that meet the needs of right and justice among men.

St. Paul clearly states in what sense government has divine sanction, when he writes, "Rulers are not a terror to good works, but to the evil. Wilt thou then not be afraid of the power? do that which is good, and thou shalt have praise of the same. For he is the minister of God to thee for good. But if thou do that which is evil, be afraid; for he beareth not the sword in vain: for he is the minister of God, a revenger to execute wrath upon him that doeth evil." Rom. 13, 3-4.

St. Peter sums it up briefly, "for the punishment of evildoers, and for the praise of them that do well." 1 Pet. 2, 14.

God's sanction of government does not imply that all forms of government are equally good and suitable for all nations. In the case of his own people Israel we see Moses and Joshua, then the judges, then kings, finally foreign dominion. The hand of God's providence is seen all through the history of nations down to the present day. No man will ever be able to trace out the workings of providence, how God blesses and how he punishes by allowing now this, now that form of government to arise for a people, now good, now evil rulers to dominate, now one kingdom to overthrow another, and itself in turn to be overthrown. Nations and rulers are in his hand. And it is just a little too vast a problem for any human mind to figure out the details of the governments of all the world according to the plans of God.

Eli the judge was weak, Samuel noble and true. King Saul ended in suicide, King David with all his faults ended well. Herod the Great was a tyrant brute and tried to kill the child Jesus. Pontius Pilate was a coward, Herod Antipas, the tetrarch, a "fox," — between them Jesus died on the cross. The Jews lost Jerusalem and Palestine, and have never regained them again. Democracies as well as kingdoms and empires, flourished and then faded and died.

Always there is government — that is God's will. There are varying forms, but the hand of providence is back of them and over them all, now to bestow national blessings, now to precipitate national ruin.

Thousands are blind. They deny, pervert, perish. It is the royal priesthood that is called to know, to realize, to bow down before God. He instituted government for man's good. We accept and use it according to his will.

This places our citizenship on the highest possible level. As priests of God we are

THE BEST POSSIBLE CITIZENS.

Two things distinguish the priests of God in their earthly citizenship. The first is that they know God's will and Word regarding earthly government. Accordingly they consider and treat it as "ordained" of God.

This is beyond all those who think government is a mere human evolution, an arrangement they have helped to make, a matter of consent between them and their fellow citizens. The lower you place government, the lower will be your citizenship and all your civic activity.

This comes most clearly to view in the second point that distinguishes the citizenship of the royal priesthood. They obey their government "for the Lord's sake," 1 Pet. 2, 13; or, as St. Paul writes, "for conscience sake," Rom. 13, 5. There can be no higher motive for submission and obedience.

Beside this highest motive St. Paul places the common low one, when he writes, "Ye must needs be subject, not only for wrath, but also for conscience sake." Note the difference. The one fears the "wrath" of the government as represented in the severity of the law and its administrators. The other rises above such fear, and responds to the voice of conscience as prompted by God.

The one is forced obedience, the other willing obedience. The one stops the moment the force compelling it ceases, or can be successfully evaded and ignored. The other goes on of its own inward accord. The one bows before the strong human hand of the government and its police, the other bows before the divine presence back of the government.

The one obedience makes for a low type citizenship, the other makes for the very highest type.

There is much complaint about increasing crime, dishonest schemes for defrauding people, burglaries, robberies, murder, and many others. What is the trouble? A citizenship uncontrolled by the Lord and conscience. A citizenship deterred only by fear, ready to laugh and mock at the arm of the law when it proves too short to reach them.

We hear much preaching on "the reverence of law," law and laws made by the government, enforced, partly enforced, perhaps left altogether unenforced by the government. What is there so sacred about this sort of law for people who think of government only as a human thing and obey government only as a force that may punish them? Mighty little indeed! Especially when courts and police connive at law transgression, become lax in law enforcement, and help to make the law weak and helpless. Idealizing "law" as a sort of sacred thing in itself is not the remedy, but putting God and conscience back of the government and its laws, and establishing only such laws and law enforcement as will tally with God and conscience.

GOD'S PRIESTS AND GOD'S GOVERNMENT

never have any difficulty with each other.

Just what is "good government" for which Luther teaches us to pray in his explanation of the fourth petition of the Lord's Prayer? St. Paul tells us in Rom. 13, 3-4, and also St. Peter in 1 Pet. 2, 14. It is a government that is a terror to evildoers, and a protection and help for all that do good.

As priests of God we will thank God for such a government, and earnestly pray for its welfare at all times. In the General Prayer in the morning service of the churches occur these significant petitions:

"Bestow the influence of Thy grace upon all the nations of the earth. We pray Thee especially to bless our land, and all its inhabitants, and all who are in authority. Cause Thy glory to dwell in our land, mercy and truth, righteousness and peace, everywhere to prevail."

St. Paul exhorts, "that first of all supplications, prayers, intercessions, and giving of thanks be made for all men; for kings and for all that are in authority, that we may lead a quiet and peaceable life in all godliness and honesty. For this is good and acceptable in the sight of God and our Savior." 1 Tim. 2, 1-3.

As priests of God we will obey the laws of our government, and do it for the Lord's sake. Even poor and faulty laws will find us obedient, though with all proper means we may try to have the faults removed.

For conscience sake we will support the government, "for for this cause pay ye tribute also: for they" (the powers that be) "are God's ministers attending continually upon this very thing," namely punishing evildoers, and helping them that do good, Rom. 13, 6.

Likewise we will honor our government. "Render therefore to all their dues: tribute to whom tribute is due; custom to whom custom; fear to whom fear; honor to whom honor." Rom. 13, 7. "Honor the king." 1 Pet. 2, 17.

It is easy for us to live happily under good government, honest, just, and efficient rulers. But how about

GOD'S PRIESTS AND EVIL GOVERNMENT?

We have the best kind of an answer, one that does not only tell us what to do, but also furnishes us the best possible examples.

Jesus was born and lived all his life under an evil government. He fled from the hand of a murderous tyrant, Herod the Great. One answer to the question is simply, Flight. We read of the saints in Heb. 11, 38, "They wandered in deserts, and in mountains, and in dens and caves of the earth," as poor fugitives. So David fled from jealous King Saul. History tells of many others.

Neither by precept or example does the Bible counsel or excuse rebellion for the royal priesthood. That is left for those who stand on a lower level as regards government. Neither Jesus nor his apostles fomented rebellion. When the thing was suggested unto the Lord he pointed to the penny stamped with Cæsar's image and superscription, and gave the famous answer, "Render therefore unto

Cæsar the things which are Cæsar's, and unto God the things which are God's." Matth. 22, 21.

If anything more is required St. Paul furnishes it in Rom. 13, 2, "Whosoever therefore resisteth the power, resisteth the ordinance of God: and they that resist shall receive to themselves damnation."

Shall we as royal priests of Christ pay taxes to a usurping or an evil government?

We have Christ's answer in his word regarding Cæsar. He bade the Jews pay taxes to the hated Roman emperor who ruled them. Then we have Jesus' example of paying for himself the Jewish Temple tax, although as Son of God and Lord of the Temple such a thing as taxing him should have been impossible. Matth. 17, 24-27.

So St. Paul also writes to the Christians at Rome, "Tribute to whom tribute is due; custom to whom custom." Christians pay taxes "for conscience sake."

Far graver is the question that arises when evil government attempts to interfere with the Gospel and our faith, and uses violence to back up its commands.

Here we have the shining example of Jesus who suffered and died under the Jewish and heathen governmental authorities. He was perfectly innocent. His trial was a travesty of justice, the outcome of a murderous plot. His sentence of crucifixion was the cowardly act of a Roman governor who knew his own criminal guilt in rendering that sentence. Jesus submitted and did not resist.

The apostles followed the same course. Peter and John went to jail for preaching the name Jesus. Their answer to the Jewish government was very simple, "Whether it be right in the sight of God to hearken unto you more than unto God, judge ye." Acts 4, 19. They went on with the preaching as before, even in the courts of the Temple. When the Twelve were thrown into jail, their answer was to same, "We ought to obey God rather than men." Acts

7, 29. They were severely whipped, threatened again, and sent away. But they did not stop their preaching.

Stephen and James, the brother of John, died like their Master.

Thus the long line of martyrs for the faith began to form. The answer of the royal priesthood to evil government forbidding the Gospel and the exercise of faith was a unanimous submission to every kind of cruel infliction down to the most excruciating forms of death. By word and example they preached the Law and the Gospel to the government officials themselves, and St. Paul reached even the emperor's own court. The one thing they did not do was to yield or even to compromise.

The story of this quiet, submissive and unshaken resistance to evil government bent on suppressing the Gospel is one of the grandest chapters in the history of the royal priesthood of Christ.

It shames so many of us in the present generation. They now would conquer by surrendering; they now would win by compromising. What if our government should forbid all use of wine, even that in the Sacrament? That question has been asked, actually asked as if the answer could for one moment be in doubt. One dreads to think of the pitiful weakness that would appear if our government should ever do what the Jewish Sanhedrim did to Peter and John, and to the Twelve.

We must now look at the long course of history and what it has brought forth on the great question of

CHURCH AND STATE.

For centuries the Bible idea of the Church as a spiritual body composed only of the royal priesthood of believers was lost. That meant also that people no longer looked for this spiritual body, or knew the marks by which to locate its presence, namely the preaching, teaching, and confession of the pure Gospel of Christ. What was supposed to be the Church was a great, powerful, outward organization under an earthly ruler, the pope at Rome, embracing all who adhered to this outward organization and gave allegiance to him.

The result in the course of history was all kinds of mixtures and entanglements between Church and State, extending down even to the present day.

At one time history shows us the Church, namely the great papal organization, supreme over all states. Kings and states humbly did the bidding of the pope. Then again history shows us the other extreme, the State dominates the Church completely in its own territory. The Church is treated as a department of the State and is managed accordingly. Between these two extremes there are various types of entanglement, according as the Church or the State may at one time or another prevail in independence.

The Reformation brought back the true Bible idea of the Church, but many rejected the Reformation and all it brought. The papacy continued as before. Even where the Reformation prevailed its true teaching concerning what the Church of Christ really is could not at once be fully put into practice. Certain entanglements between Church and State still went on, even increased, right in the home of the Reformation, and are not removed to this day.

Not until our own Republic was established, with its great principle of complete separation between Church and State, was the Church free to stand wholly alone. The entanglements are broken. The Church is able to develop freely according to its own inherent power. Nobody has a right to interfere with its inward spiritual work or its outward management.

It is this

COMPLETE SEPARATION BETWEEN CHURCH AND STATE

which alone comports fully with the royal priesthood of believers as taught in the Bible. In fact, it is the royal priesthood which in principle demands such a separation. The real reason for such a separation is grounded in the Bible teaching concerning the royal priesthood and man's direct accountability to God for everything that pertains to his soul.

No government, no matter what it may claim as its authority, whether it be theocratic, i.e. combine civil and ecclesiastical power, like the old Sanhedrim of the Jews, or whether it be secular only, like the power of the Roman governor Pontinus Pilate, has a right to interfere with us as priests of God in our religion.

This is the full implication of St. Peter's word when he told the Jewish Sanhedrim for himself and St. John, "Whether it be right in the sight of God to hearken unto you more than unto God, judge ye." Acts 4, 19. Likewise when the Twelve told the Sanhedrim, "We ought to obey God rather than men." Acts 7, 29. By thus refusing to bow to any other authority in matters of the Gospel, faith, and its exercise, except to the authority of God, the divine rights of the royal priesthood were maintained by the apostles, and at the same time all human government was put in its proper place. It must leave the royal priesthood, which is the true Church, alone in matters of religion.

That means separation of Church and State.

The entire history of the early Christian Church stands for this principle. The Church acts on it, and is ready to suffer for it. Roman emperors and governors forbade Christianity as a *religio illicita*, an illicit or unlawful religion. Punishment even unto the most cruel death was made the penalty. But, like the apostles, the royal priest-hood of those early believers refused to obey. In all civil and secular matters they gladly obeyed, not in this divine matter of religion and the Gospel. That meant that the government had no right to interfere with religion. Or, in other words, Church and State should be separate.

We see how this separation is demanded by the very nature of the royal priesthood. But the thing goes farther. The right we must demand for ourselves to practice our religion ought to be extended to all our fellow citizens in the same way, no matter what their religious convictions may be. Their religion may be false in part or altogether. For that they are answerable to God alone. It is no busi-ness of the government at all. The work of the government lies in a different direction altogether. Its sphere is secular and civil, as St. Peter puts it, "for the punishment of evildoers, and for the praise of them that do well." 1 Pet. 2, 14.

As far as the religious teaching and practices of the citizens are concerned the government has only one thing to say, namely that no citizen shall teach or practice, under the plea of religion, anything that is contrary to natural right and justice. If I teach murder, adultery, or stealing, the government has a right to stop me. I may say that such teaching is my religion. The government's answer is, We do not care what your religion is, your teaching is contrary to all human right and justice, and for that reason criminal. There is practically no difficulty in drawing the line. Religious and secular matters are easily kept apart.

It is the State's great work to attend to all things civil and secular. It is the work of the Church, and of the religious organizations commonly called "churches," to attend to all things spiritual and religious.

The State regulates the relation of one citizen to another in all matters of civil right and justice. The Church, and

religious bodies, regulate the relation of their members
to God.

When each attends to its own proper sphere, and avoids
interference, both will profit in the highest degree.

Yet we must add that while these two spheres are distinct
and separate, they stand side by side and touch each
other in various natural ways.

The power of the State protects its citizens, not only
when they follow their secular work, but also when they
practice their religion. We are free to build churches,
schools, parish houses, colleges, seminaries, and institu-
tions of mercy, and no one dare put anything in our
way. We may freely assemble to hear the Gospel preached
and to worship God in public services. In fact, the State
recognizes the benefit of religion to the citizenship in general. It thus leaves church property untaxed, and by law
makes Sunday a day of rest throughout its territory.

There is the same friendly contact on the part of the
Church with the State. We pray for our government, obey
its laws, seek its welfare in all proper ways. The true
Church teaches all men the divine sanctions on which the
State rests. By instilling true religion and morality the
Church maintains the moral standards which the State
needs so much but cannot itself provide. The Church
promotes conscientious action by the citizens, in particular
also over against the State. It is surely a great help
to the government when its citizens, with St. Paul, look
upon it as "the minister of God" (Rom. 13, 4 and 6) to
be obeyed "for the Lord's sake" (1 Pet. 2, 13).

Yet in these helpful contacts there is not, need not and
should not be, any intermingling of Church and State,
which would always be harmful.

A government that remains in its own proper sphere is
a great blessing for the royal priesthood of Christ. We
surely ought to prize it and pray constantly for its con-
tinuance. A Church that remains in its proper sphere is

a great blessing for the State and its citizens. The State ought to prize such a Church and put no hindrance in its way.

Thank God that his providence has given us a good government of this kind! Yet many of our citizens are not satisfied. There are church organizations which constantly attempt to mix into the affairs of the government, in fact consider it their duty to do so. They try to dictate policies, laws, and certain kinds of law enforcements to the government. They try to influence and control elections. At times government officials also attempt to go beyond their sphere. They try to use the Church for political affairs which are no concern of the Church at all.

All attempts, movements, and tendencies which seek to erase the line between Church and State threaten harm to both, and must be steadily resisted. Good statesmanship will make this resistance for sound political reasons, which certainly have great weight. But the most powerful motive for keeping Church and State separate lies in the divinely established royal priesthood of believers whose supreme law is God and God's Word alone.

As the royal priesthood, in standing for the supreme interests of the soul in its relation to God, originally furnished the real and effective principle for separation of Church and State, so this royal priesthood will ever continue to furnish that principle. And all God's kings and priests who have the full light of his Word in their hearts will do their utmost to have that principle put into the most perfect practice.

Kings and Priests — Tears and Blood

This is the bloody chapter on the royal priesthood. And, of course, blood and tears go together.

There has to be a chapter like this, or the royal priesthood would not be what we have said of it thus far and what the Lord God intended that it should be.

Yet it would be an utter misconception to read this chapter as a presentation of the sad side of the royal priesthood. No, no! While it is about tears and blood, weeping, heartbreak, and martyrdom, this is really *the glory chapter* on the royal priesthood.

There is no more royal deed a spiritual king unto God can do than to lay down his life for the faith. There is no higher priestly deed a spiritual priest unto God can do than to bring his own life as an offering and sacrifice unto God. And when the great opportunity comes to any of our kings and priests to rise unto such heights, there is no cause for lament, but for the praise of God whose grace is able to raise such poor mortals as us to such exaltation in his kingdom.

We may begin with Jesus himself. It is he who holds out to all his followers

THE ATTRACTION OF TEARS AND BLOOD.

Right in the start, in the great Sermon on the Mount, the Lord makes this the climax of the Beatitudes, the crowning one of them all, "Blessed are ye, when men shall revile you, and persecute you, and shall say all manner of evil against you, for my sake. Rejoice and be exceeding glad; for great is your reward in heaven: for so persecuted they the prophets which were before you." Matth. 5, 11-12.

Or take it in the other version, "Blessed are ye, when men shall hate you, and when they shall separate you from their company, and shall reproach you, and cast out your name as evil, for the Son of man's sake. Rejoice ye in that day, and leap for joy: for, behold, your reward is great in heaven: for in like manner did their fathers unto the prophets." Luke 6, 22-23. In verse 26 St. Luke adds the reverse, "Woe unto you, when all men shall speak well of you! for so did their fathers to the false prophets."

The Beatitudes are blessings, and blessings are always held out in order to attract, not to repel. Only woes are meant to repel.

There is only one way by which common mortals like ourselves may enter the royal company of the prophets who died for the faith. It is the avenue of tears and blood.

But how can tears and blood in a real way be considered attractions? Are they not in reality drawbacks, evils instead of blessings? In answer we might point to any hero in battle. All men deem his death glorious.

But the Lord himself gives us the answer, and it is even better than the one touched upon. "Great is your reward in heaven!" he tells us. Tears and blood for Christ's sake endure but a short time; then comes the heavenly reward of grace which shall for ever make us the companions of men like Elijah, Isaiah, Jeremiah, St. Peter, St. Paul, St. James, and the rest.

St. John had a vision of this noble company in heaven, "And I saw thrones, and they that sat upon them, and judgment was given unto them: and I saw the souls of them that were beheaded for the witness of Jesus, and for the Word of God." Rev. 20, 4.

Read again some of the promises made by the Lord to them that overcome.

"To him that overcometh will I give to eat of the tree of life, which is in the midst of the Paradise of God." Rev. 2, 7. "He that overcometh shall not be hurt of the second death." V. 11. "To him that overcometh will I give to eat of the hidden manna, and will give him a white stone, and in the stone a new name written, which no man knoweth saving he that receiveth it." V. 17.

"He that overcometh, and keepeth my works unto the end, to him will I give power over the nations: And he shall rule them with a rod of iron; as the vessels of a potter shall they be broken into shivers: even as I received of my Father. And I will give him the morning star." V. 26-28.

"He that overcometh, the same shall be clothed in white raiment; and I will not blot out his name out of the book of life, but I will comfess his name before my Father, and before his angels." Rev. 3, 5. "Him that overcometh will I make a pillar in the temple of my God, and he shall go no more out: and I will write upon him the name of God, and the name of the city of my God, which is new Jerusalem, which cometh down out of heaven from my God: and I will write upon him my new name." V. 12.

"To him that overcometh will I grant to sit with me in my throne, even as I also overcame, and am set down with my Father in his throne." V. 21. "He that overcometh shall inherit all things; and I will be his God, and he shall be my son." Rev. 21, 7.

Of course, it takes a royal and priestly soul to see this glory, and at the prospect of it to "rejoice and be exceeding glad" and "leap for joy," as the Lord puts it. But this is exactly what the grace of God achieves in the souls of the royal priesthood, namely work an appreciation of the imperishable glory of the cross. St. Paul writes for them, "We glory in tribulation also." Rom. 5, 3.

Nor are these words only. The Twelve were scourged by the Jewish Sanhedrim, but they left "rejoicing that they were counted worthy to suffer shame for his (Christ's) name." St. Paul himself endured all kinds of violent persecution, but he tells us, "I take pleasure in persecutions, in distress for Christ's sake." 2 Cor. 12, 10. With a martyr's death in immediate prospect, he writes to his friend Timothy, "There is laid up for me a crown of righteousness." 2 Tim. 4, 8. How the Lord looks upon these royal priests who thus suffered tears and blood for his name and Gospel the letter to the Hebrews 11, 38 tells us, "Of whom the world was not worthy."

In all this story of tears and blood the royal priesthood takes on the semblance of Christ, our great Exemplar. When he was strongly reminded of his death he said, "The hour is come that the Son of man should be glorified." John 12, 23. And in the very night in which he was betrayed he said to his disciples, "Now is the Son of man glorified." John 13, 31. He was King and High Priest, and the glory of both of these high offices is in the shame and death they brought to him on Golgotha. As the great Captain of our salvation he was made "perfect through suffering," Heb. 2, 10, an High Priest after the order of Melchizedek, Heb. 5, 9-10. Even in heaven this is his glory that he is the Lamb that was slain, that he was dead and yet liveth for ever. Rev. 1, 18.

Blood and tears often become the test of our royal priesthood. St. Peter writes of it, "That the trial of your faith, being much more precious than of gold that perisheth, though it be tried with fire, might be found unto praise and honor and glory at the appearing of Jesus Christ." 1 Pet. 1, 7. St. James does the same, "Blessed is the man that endureth temptation: for when he is tried, he shall receive the crown of life, which the Lord hath promised to them that love him." James 1, 12.

Fair weather Christians are not genuine. It is the wormy fruit that falls in a storm. Jesus tells us, the wheat on stony ground withers away when the sun is up, because it has no root. Matth. 13, 6.

When we read these things about tears and blood, about the lesser and the greater sufferings of the royal priesthood for the sake of the Gospel, it almost seems as if this were the normal thing. It is the worst possible abnormality, as the Bible itself shows us by describing

THE FOUNTAIN OF TEARS AND BLOOD.

Men who love and worship the true God in the way he himself has ordained, who love to do good to all men for Christ's sake, and who are loyal to government for conscience sake, surely ought to be admired, praised, favored, and rewarded by all who come into contact with them. Who could find any just cause for interfering with them or harassing them?

But this unreasonable and outrageous treatment is exactly what Christ foretold and what has actually come to pass. Here is what Jesus said, "If the world hate you, ye know that it hated me before it hated you. If ye were of the world, the world would love its own: but because ye are not of the world, but I have chosen you out of the world, therefore the world hateth you." John 15, 18-19. Nor does this apply only to the early days of the Church, for Jesus says of the time preceding the end, "Then shall they deliver you up to be afflicted, and shall kill you; and ye shall be hated of all nations for my name's sake." Matth. 24, 9.

The fountain of tears and blood for the royal priesthood is the world. All the sin and wickedness in it, all the opposition to God and the true religion, and all the love of religious lies and perversions, in many ways, and especially at certain times, send forth a bitter hostility against the royal priesthood which confesses and practices the true religion. This fountain is deep and strong, and is bound to send out a great stream of acrid water.

It is the mighty hand of Providence which in spite of this hostility grants to his true Church times of peace and refreshment. For these we ought to be exceedingly thankful. Yet we should know that when all seems serene and secure there is a deep undercurrent in the world which may break forth at any time and send out anew a flood of tears and blood over the loyal confessors of the royal priesthood.

The pages of history are black with the records of persecution. There were ten great waves of suffering and blood in the first centuries under the heathen Empire of Rome. In the Middle Ages and on past the era of the Reformation there looms up the iniquitous papal Inquisition with its frightful infliction of cruel tortures and long train of executions. Lea required two large volumes for the Inquisition alone. How many more would it take to record all the intolerance, disabilities, fines, confiscations, degradations, forced exile, repressive laws, and other inflictions, which all have been used to suppress the true religion and men's efforts to attain it? Every device that cunning and violence could invent has been employed.

Even in recent days missionaries have paid with their lives for their holy work. The martyrdom of Christian pastors and people during the revolutionary upheaval in Russia and the Baltic provinces as a sequel of the world war is a heartrending story known all too little in spite of our great press associations, which are more interested in secular things. In our own land of religious liberty the keenest weapons of the mind are constantly wielded against the saving truth of Christ and those who profess that truth. Often enough in a quiet way painful damage is inflicted on those who are faithful to their Lord. Their income, good name and character, advancement and standing is made to suffer. The old hostility is there. If it cannot get blood it will take tears at least, heartaches and distress of any kind. All it needs is a good opportunity. Though the civil laws demand tolerance, attempts to change them back to the old vicious intolerance are renewed from time to time.

This hostility to the royal priesthood and what it stands for has been one continuous effort for

THE COERCION OF CONSCIENCE.

You and I are not to be free to worship the dictates of our own consciences; somebody else wants to dictate to us and force our consciences. Human authorities in the guise of the State, or of the Church, or of a combination of the two; and where these fail, human authorities in the guise of learning, science, liberalism, modernism, spurious progressivism, try to override the true faith, crush it out, and chain conscience to their own religious or anti-religious ideas.

The resistance to these despicable efforts forms the most glorious chapter in the history of Christ's confessors in the royal priesthood. It has been almost always, as it also should be, a passive resistance, a simple refusal to yield the conscience, coupled with a readiness to endure the worst that its opponents could inflict. Of course, many have been swept away in the trial of faith, too weak to endure unto the end, to attain to the great triumph in what outwardly looked to men like defeat.

As one goes over the pages of history he is surprised, how exceedingly long it has taken for the royal priesthood to win general recognition among men, in particular also in the laws of the more enlightened governments, recognition of the great principle of

LIBERTY OF CONSCIENCE

for Christ's confessors and for all men generally.

Liberty of conscience is so clearly voiced in the New Testament. St. Peter and St. John actually gave it classic expression when they told the Jewish rulers who tried to coerce their consciences, "Whether it be right in the sight of God to hearken unto you more than unto God, judge ye." Acts 4, 19. The Twelve shortly after put it still more effectively before the same tribunal, "We ought to obey God rather than men." Acts 5, 29. Now the spirit of these decisive declarations for liberty of conscience never died altogether in the history of the Church, but there were long periods when it was surely submerged. For ages the Church herself stooped to the heathen weapon of coercion, which it should never have used. Instead of acclaiming liberty of conscience, any assertion of it was put down whenever possible, and the cry for such liberty was stifled. Always a host of human authorities and powers crowded in between God and the souls of men that tried to reach God by means of his Word alone. Even to own that Word was at times branded as a capital crime.

Really it was not till that great day broke when Martin Luther, a lone monk, faced the Diet at Worms in Germany with the Emperor Charles V. and all the dignitaries of the Church and State, that the voice of the apostles was again raised with full clearness and courage demanding liberty of conscience. The assembled civil and ecclesiastical authorities demanded that this monk should, without further question or argument, recant and retract all his writings and submit his conscience to them. He asked time to consider his answer. On the day following, facing the entire imposing array, he made this reply.

"Unless I be convinced by testimonies of Scripture or clear reasons — for I believe neither the pope nor the councils alone, since it is evident, they have often erred and contradicted themselves, — I am convinced by the Sacred Scriptures I have quoted, and my conscience is bound in God's Word. I can recant nothing, and will recant nothing, because it is unsafe and dangerous to act against conscience!" And then a moment later, "Here I stand. I cannot do otherwise. God help me!"

Thus Luther, like the twelve apostles of old, stood like a rock, unshaken, for the liberty of conscience — a conscience bound by the Word of God alone. We are gripped by the heroism of his act. But its importance exceeds the heroism of the man himself. On the principle of a conscience free from all human authority and resting on God alone Luther's entire work was founded.

Of course, the Diet granted no such liberty either to Luther or any other man. The very idea of such liberty was an incomprehensible thing to those who heard his reply. Luther was banned and excommunicated.

The Lord allowed the Reformation to spread in spite of the intolerant forces arrayed against it. It won its way far and wide. And yet the thing that one would expect, namely that the great liberty for which Luther stood as a lone hero at Worms would at once be fully established wherever the Reformation came into complete control, this very thing was not realized. State as well as Church laws kept withholding and denying religious freedom. One had to believe and worship as the laws required in the kingdom or province in which he happened to live; if he refused he was expelled.

Something was gained — he only had to migrate, he was

not tortured and killed. It was a long way to the goal set by St. Peter and St. John. This ought to show us how precious the treasure is, now that it has been made ours at last.

Full religious liberty, freedom of conscience, and the right freely to worship God as one's own heart dictates, was not attained until the American colonies were formed and our Republic was organized. In 1636 Roger Williams proclaimed this basic law in the colony of Rhode Island. Maryland followed in 1649. William Penn did the same in 1682, granting the widest liberties. More than a century later, in 1791, the Constitution of the United States made complete religious liberty the universal law of our land. Europe lagged behind. Not till the nineteenth century was reached and half gone, did most of the European governments adopt religious liberty in their legal systems, and even now in a few cases there are restrictions.

The Church as well as the nations were slow to cash in on the great legacy of Luther's declaration of religious independence made at Worms in 1521, April 18.

In conclusion let us look somewhat more closely at

THE BLESSING OF FREE CONSCIENCES.

Conscience is really man's own soul sitting in judgment on his own motives, intentions, and acts, either to approve them as right, or to disapprove them as wrong. It is conscience that makes man a moral and religious being.

While conscience always distinguishes some things as right and some things as wrong, it does not of itself possess the infallible norm for truly deciding what is right and what is wrong. There is only one such norm, namely God's own Word. All other norms are misleading, some of them terribly so.

Conscience itself cannot be coerced. It will in the end declare right only what it deems right, and vice versa. It will do this even against man's own will, and certainly against any other will that would attempt coercion.

But conscience can be tyrranized. That means, a man can be forced to call wrong what the verdict of his conscience must call right, or call right what his conscience condemns as wrong. Likewise he can be forced to do wrong against the verdict of his conscience, or prevented from doing right against the same verdict. Thus to violate conscience is to outrage man's moral and religious nature.

When now the royal priesthood stood up in the persons of the twelve apostles, and again in Martin Luther, protesting against this outrage, and demanding the right to obey God alone in all things religious, it stood up, not merely for itself as demanding an exceptional privilege, but equally for all men, demanding liberty of conscience for them all. As there dare be no tyranny over my soul and conscience, so there dare be no tyranny over any man's.

But how when men's consciences do not bow to God and his Word? How when they are misled by false norms and by ignorance of the right norm? Right here is where the evil has crept in. When men thought others were going astray, by believing, living, and worshipping wrongly, they thought they were entitled to step in and use force. Often they imagined that by thus using force they were doing God service. John 16, 2. It was thus that tyranny justified itself. It imagined it was bestowing a blessing, though it was by force.

The right answer is not force or any form of violence. Luther has reiterated again and again that the battles for men's souls and consciences are not for the sword of steel, but for the Sword of the Spirit, which is the Word of God. Eph. 6, 17. There is only one right way to set men's consciences right, and that is the divine way.

Mohammedanism converts by the sword, Christianity by the Gospel.

While it is true that the soul of itself does not possess the divine norm of right for its perfect guidance, it does possess a limited natural sense of right and wrong. Even heathen nations have established civil justice. By means of a kind of natural law in their hearts men praise and cultivate certain natural virtues and condemn and punish common vices and crimes. It is for this reason that government passes laws and enforces them by police power. Only, natural morality is weak, superficial, and often altogether faulty. Yet crime and vice are rightly punished by the strong arm of the law, no matter what the blind consciences of the vicious may say, or human society would be wrecked. St. Paul himself wrote that the government does not bear the sword in vain. Rom. 13, 4.

This, however, is a different thing entirely from making men religious by force, compelling them to practice some form of worship, even though it be of the true religion, by means of threats and penalties; or preventing them from exercising some form of religion, either true or false. To do this sort of thing is itself the worst form of crime.

What a blessing then for all of us, whoever we may be, to be free from all tyranny of conscience! The God who gave you your soul gave you a conscience in and with that soul. For that soul, and in that conscience, you are responsible to him alone. Let no human power then interfere with that soul and conscience by threats and violence. Let God come to you, God alone, with his Word, its light and love, its grace and gifts, to enlighten, free, and uplift your soul to communion with God.

We of the royal priesthood who have experienced this heavenly power from God know what blessedness it always brings. And the one thing we ask, and ever must ask, is that our souls and consciences, and those of all men alike, be left free to attain and enjoy their blessedness.

By no force that men have ever invented can this true blessedness be made theirs. The Gospel is the only power of salvation. Faith is the key, not force.

If men's consciences cannot be reached by God, then there is no hope for them. If God fails, men cannot succeed.

Yet we of the royal priesthood must not think that when liberty of conscience is secured for us by the very law of the State, no effort will be made at coercing us in religious things. There will always be ways and means for some kind of antichristian pressure against the faith. The world will never be so arranged that the kings and priests of Christ will get through it unscathed and un-scarred, without shedding some tears and leaving some blood.

We are kings and priests unto God. Let that be our joy and holy pride. The more we realize what our royal priesthood really is, the more will we prize the priceless blessings it has brought for us, and, connected with these blessings, the precious benefactions it has scattered abroad in all the world.

SOLI DEO GLORIA!